URBAN POLLUTION
ISSUES AND SOLUTIONS

URBAN POLLUTION
ISSUES AND SOLUTIONS

Editors

A. ARYA
S. J. BEDI
Y. T. JASRAI
V. S. PATEL

NIDHI BOOK CENTRE
DELHI (INDIA)

First Published : 2005

Published by
NIDHI BOOK CENTRE
3421-A, IInd Floor, Narang Colony, Tri Nagar,
Delhi-35. Ph. : 2739 3083, 3096 7505 (O) , 2752 2129 (R)

ISBN : 81-902086-2-4

Laser Type Setting by
A-ONE GRAPHICS
JD-18C, IInd Floor, Pitampura, Delhi-110088

Printed at
BDH Printer at Salasar Imaging System, Delhi.

Contents

Preface

The major pollutants like particulate matter, VOCs, CO, NO_x, SO_x are called **Primary pollutants.** When fuels and wastes are burnt, praticles consisting mainly of carbon are emitted into the air: these are the praticulate we see in form of soot and smoke. Some of the primary pollutants may undergo further changes to produce secondary pollutants, these are called **secondary pollutants.** Some of these are ozone, PANs, sulphur and nitric acids. According to EPA data, (1996) emissions in the United States of America the first five primary pollutants amounted to 154 million tonnes. Suspended particulate matter can impair many respiratory functions, VOCs including gasoline and paint solvents etc. are prime agents of Ozone formation. Carbon monoxide blocks deli-very of oxygen to organs and tissues thus being harmful. Many chemical pollutants are potential carcinogens. Lead can lead to brain damage and death. Urban towns or cities are increasing with time, mushrooming industries are formed and towering, multisto-ried buidings are creating concreate jungles. What happend on the night of 2-3rd December 1984 to Bhopal can happen in any city like Baroda, Vapi, Mumbai or Chennai. The inhabitants of city use vehicles and it has been found that two or four wheelers are responsible for 80% of the air pollution, Name of **Rachel Carson** a marine scientist needs special mention because it was her book **Silent Spring** that broke the conspiracy of silence on the worldwide use of large amount of pesticides.

The basic question that a healthy mind lives in a healthy body can not be achieved if we live in these polluted cities. Our traditional life style and ancient wisdom was mixed with harmony of nature, which is tragically lost with the present setup. Gone are the days, when we used to listen chirping of birds in the morning or have cattles in our houses. Now poor fellow dog is our lone companion and sometimes this dog even forgets to bark or wave its small tail in our response. The world's most livable cities are not those with perfect auto acccess between all points. For example Geneva, Switzerland prohibits automobile parking at workplaces in city, forcing commuters to use the excellent public transportation system. Copenhagen bans all on street parking in the downtown core. Paris has removed 200,000 parking places in the downtown area. In Tokyo, millions of people still ride bicycle either all the way to work or stations from which they catch efficient subways or Bullet train.

With this back drop, a National seminar was organized by **Indian Association for Air Pollution Control (IAAPC)** on 22nd March 2003 in Vadodara, to discuss **Issues related to** Urban Pollution and their Solutions. Twenty four speakers presented their original research papers in two different sessions. Papers related to varied subjects like Aerodynamics of Vehicles, Clean car standards, Eco-friendly lighting design, Assessment of pollutants on crops, Biological filtration of indoor air, An efficient method to detect the pollution load in indoor area, Pollution in city of Taj etc. Now is the age of developing **Sustainable Cities,** some 100 countires have developed their own National Environmental action Plans. Thus there is emphasis on maintaining the forest cover, produce green belts and parks and gardens in cities, making judicious use of available natural resources, adopt the technologies like rain water harvesting or use of wind energy for various purposes. Special attention is being paid so that flora and fauna is not lost. Vertical growth of cities may be alowed but with required safety and better enviroment norms. There is a need of establishment of a continuing environmental planning and management process. The papers presented during Seminar generated lot of enthusiasm, we hope the articles presented in this volume will be helpful to readers and researchers in the field.

We are really thankful to all the contributors of this book for attending the Seminar and allowing us to print these in form of a book. We are grateful to Prof. H.V. Bhavnani, Past President of IAAPC, Prof. N.M. Bhatt and Dr. S.S. Bala, CPCB (West Zone) for their help. Our sincere thanks are due to Shri C.P. Gautam of Nidhi Publications for nice printing of the book.

9th April, 2005
Vadodara.

A. Arya
S. J. Bedi
Y. T. Jasrai
V. S. Patel

List of Figures

List of Colour Plates

Pl. 4 A. Petri dishes showing growth of *Rhizopus* in one and in another bacteria and fungi are present in Egypto-babylonian Gallery

B. Part of strip containing SCA medium showing growth of Bacteria present in Egyptobabylonian Gallery.

Article 17

Pl. 1. *Aeglonema*

Pl. 2. *Sansevieria*

Pl. 3. *Chrysanthemum*

Pl. 4. *Dracena*

Article 18

Pl.1 A. Healthy shoots of *Ficus religiosa* growing in MS medium

B. Explants showing growth of *Fusarium oxysporum.*

C. Growth of *A. flavus* associated with explants.

D. Growth of black coloured mycelium of *Thielaviopsis* state of *Ceratocystis paradoxa.*

Pl.2. A. Growth of *F. oxysporum* in one of the explants.

B. Bacterial growth near one explant and growth of *Alternaria infectoria* near another explants.

C. Growth of *F. oxysporum* in one of the explants.

Article 19

Pl. 1. Role of such trees for making cities better liven up.

A. *Butea monosperma*

B. *Manilkara hexandra*

C. *Azadirachta indica*

D. *Acacia nilotica*

E. *Thespesia populena*

Pl. 2. Role of such trees for making cities better liven up.

A. *Ficus benghalensis*

B. *Tectona grandis*

C. *Anogeissus sericea*

D. *Mimusops elengi*

List of Contributors

Arun Arya

Botany Department, Faculty of Science, The M.S. University of Baroda, Vadodara 390002

E-Mail: aryaarunarya@rediffmail.com.

Anjali Pahad

Sr. Lecturer, Department of Home Science, Extension and Commnication, Faculty of Home Science, The M.S. University of Baroda, Vadodara-390002

Avani Maniar

Lecturer, Department of Hose Science Extension and Commnication, Faculty of Home Science, The M.S. University of Baroda, Vadodara-390002

Anupam Deb Sarkar

Lecturer, Environmental Engineering Section Department of Civil Engineering, Jadavpur University, Jadavpur-700032

Biswajit Thakur

Research Fellow, Environmental Engineering Section Department of Civil Engineering, Jadavpur University, Jadavpur-700032

Bindoo Bhatt

Sr. Lecturer, Department of Geography, Faculty of Science, The M.S. University of Baroda, Vadodara-390002

Chitra Arya

Botany Department, Faculty of Science, The M.S. University of Baroda, Vadodara-390002

E-Mail: aryachitraarya@yahoo.com.

C. Patvardhan

Faculty of Engineering, Dayalbagh Educational Institite, Agra-282005

Chinmoyee Dash

Botany Department, Faculty of Science, The M.S. University of Baroda, Vadodara-390002

Divya Ajwani

Lecturer, Depatment of Home Management Feculty of Home Science, The M.S.U. of Baroda, Vadodara-390002

Divyang Trivedi

Student of Environmental Science,Faculty of Science M.S. University of Baroda, Vadodara-390002

G. Raja

Lecturer, Automobile Engg. Dept., Hindustan College of Engg., Padur, Kelambakkam, Chennai-603 103.

H.V. Bhavnani

Hon. Director, Parul Institute of Engineering and Tech. P.O. Limda, Ta-Vaghodia, Vadodra-391760

Indranil Mukherjee

P.G. Student, Environmental Engineering Section Department of Civil Engineering, Jadavpur University, Jadavpur-700 032

Jobi Charian

Student of Environmental Science, The M.S. University of Baroda, Vadodara, 390002

Jogender Singh

Visiting Teacher of Environmental Science, The M.S. University of Baroda, Vadodara-390002

K. Balagurunathan

Director (Acad.) St. Peter's Engineering College, College road, Avadi, Chennai-600054

K.N. Thaker

Department of Botany, Faculty of Science, The M.S. University of Baroda, Vadodara-390 002

M.N. Ahmed

Department of Chemistry, Faculty of Science, The M.S. University of Baroda, Vadodara-390 002

M.N. Thaker

Department of Biochemistry, The Maharaja Sayajirao University of Baroda, Vadodara-390 002

M. Radha Krishna

Technical College, D.E.I., Dayalbagh Educational Institute, Agra-282005

M. Subramanian

Senior Lecturer, Automobile Engg. Dept., Hindustan College of Engg., Padur, Kelambakkam, Chennai-3.

Mona Mehta

Lecturer, Department of Home Management Feculty of The Home Science, Aharaja Sayajirao University of Baroda, Vadodara-390002

N.R. Shah

Museology Department, Faculty of Fine Arts, The M.S. University of Baroda, Vadodara-390 002

E-Mail: nareshshah_1979@yahoo.com

Neena Jaju

Sr. Lecturer in Home Management, Faculty of Home

Science, The M.S. University of Baroda, Vadodara-390002

Navin Kumar Sharma

Department of Environment Studies, School of Life Science, Dr. B.R.A. University, Khandari Campus Agra-282002 (U.P.)

Parvez Vora

Student of Environmental Science, Faculty of Science, The M.S. University of Baroda, Vadodara-390002

Premendra Singh Sisodia

Department of Botany, The M.S. University of Baroda, Vadodara-390 002

P.S. Dubey

Chairman, M.P. Pollution Control Board, Paryavaran Parisar E-5 Arera Colony Bhopal (M.P.)

E-Mail: preshdubey@satyamnet.in

R.N. Ram (Late)

Department of Chemistry, Faculty of Science, The M.S. University of Baroda, Vadodara-390 002

Ranjit Singh

Faculty of Engineering, Dayalbagh Educational Institute, Agra-282005 (U.P.)

R.B. Singh

Department of Zoology, School of Life Science, Dr. B.R. Ambedkar University, Agra-282 002

S. Bhagwantha Rao

Dayalbagh Educational Institute, Agra.

Shibnath Chakrabarty

Reader, Environmental Engineering Section Department of Civil Engineering, Jadavpur University, Jadavpur-32

Timir R. Shah

Choksi Laboratories Limited, C-1 B/829, GIDC Makarpura, Vadodara-390 010

E-Mail: choksilab @ sancharnet.in

Vinod S. Patel, President-IAAPC, Ami apartment 1 Race course circle, Vadodara-390015

Y.T. Jasrai

Department of Botany, Faculty of Science, The M.S. University of Baroda, Vadodara-390002

E-Mail: yjasrai@yahoo.com

1

Urban Air Pollution and its Management

P.S. Dubey

The poisoned air indoors

In the absence of integrated abatement strategies, increased air polluation will pose an even greater threat to the health and well-being of India's urban populations, eventually under-cutting the prospects for further economic growth. Dynamic partnerships among government, industry, and the public will be crucial in making air quality management a part of urban development plans across India. Urban Air pollution is a matter of high priority in its most affected cities. In order to devise effective intervention measures, however, we need to understand which sources are responsible for the high exposure of the general public to air pollution.

Traditional fuels in rural areas are the single biggest source. Think of a woman inside a mud hut, bent over her 'chulha' or earthen oven. Imagine the amount of noxious fume that she inhales, with the oven belching smoke inside the hut. As a result of breathing in all that smoke, threats to her health could range from dizziness, headache, nausea and weakness to respiratory and heart diseases, and cancers.

The outdoors is no better

And what about air pollution levels outdoors? According

to the report, in most of the 23 Indian cities with a population of over a million, suspended particulate matter (SPM) levels (polluting elements in the air) are dangerously high.

Indian cities are among the most polluted in the world for their air pollution levels. There are too many cars and too many industries belching out fumes. Cities like Ankaleshwar, and Surat in Gujarat, Delhi, Alwar in Rajasthan, Howrah in West Bengal and the Union Territory of Pondicherry are feared to have exceeded pollution limits. This means it is positively dangerous to live in these cities; their residents run the risk of contacting numerous diseases related to pollution.

Ambient Air Quality Status derived from a network of 290 stations covering 90 towns/ cities in recent years indicates that while SPM is consistenly critical in many cities, the concentration of NOx, and SOx, is also increasing and is already transiting from Moderate to High to Critical Levels.

The industrial units in India have largely been concentrated in the States of Gujarat, Maharashtra, UP, Bihar, West Bengal and MP. The highest concentration of SOx and NOx, is therefore, often found in cities located there. Obviously, new industrial estates in Delhi, Punjab, Rajasthan, Andhra Pradesh are also manifesting a disturbing upward trend in air pollution. **Air pollution is the sum total of pollutants contributed by Transport, Industry and Power sectors.**

Fine particulates : A Silent killer

Particulate matter is the most serious pollutant in large cities in India. There are many sources of particulate pollution: large industrial plants, medium-and small-scale industries, refuse burning, households burning biomass for cooking and heating, vehicular exhaust, re-suspended road dust, construction, particles migrating from other regions, and naturally occurring dust. These sources emit particles of varying sizes- small particles affect public health much more than large particles. Particulate matter has been treated as a criteria pollutant ever since concern for air pollution was felt by society. Almost two decades ago it was realized that all of the total suspended particulates (TSP) is not harmful and health effects of particulates were more likely to be associated with finer respirable fraction. It is primarily the problem of urban areas arising from multiple sources.

Particulate Matter (PM) originates from a variety of sources, including diesel trucks, power plants, wood stoves and industrial processes. The chemical and physical composition of these various particles vary widely. While individual particles can not be seen with naked eye, collectively they can appear as black soot, dust clouds, or gray hazes.

The link between ambient PM and health effects is further complicated because of the large uncertainty in the relationship between ambient PM concentrations and actual human exposure. Identifying the PM 2.5 characteristics and / or sources that cause negative health effects requires a comprehensive data set of PM 2.5 measurements and epidemiological data. **Such a data set does not exist in our country.**

Discussion with practitioners in air quality monitoring suggest that quality assurance and quality control needs strengthening. The areas that call for attention include not only the accuracy and reproducibility of the measurements but also data analysis; timely publication of, and access to, raw data; re-examination of site selection in light of changes in land use patterns; the actual monitoring frequency; and the positioning of the instruments at a given site. With respect to how data are used, there is often a tendency to collect data at "hot spots," and to base citywide policies on the data collected at sites that rank among the most polluted. However, such an approach is not optimal for addressing air pollution at the least cost to society.

This forms the foundation for those concepts related to fine particulates in urban atmosphere, as there is **'No Escape'**. Tiny particles that cannot be seen are cutting our lives shorter.

Indian scenario for the assessment of fine particulates, its varitaion and fluctuation in air pollutant concentration with respect to time and space is of fundamental importance and basically aimed to obtain background data, trend evaluation, criteria evaluation, source detection and air pollution abatement. The effective, efficient and economic control of air quality variables requires reliable and timely information about the status of ambient air quality and its variations towards planning for prevention and control of abatement of air pollution, to safeguard the health of urban population.

The Air Quality Assessment, Environmental Damage Assessment and Abatement Options Assessment provide input to the Cost Benefit or Cost Effectiveness Analysis, which is also based on established Air Quality Objectives (i.e. guidelines, standards) and Economic Objectives (i.e. reduction of damage costs). The final result of this analysis is Optimum Control Strategy.

Impact on Crops :

Air quality in India is steadily deteriorating and in industrial pockets of the country air pollution levels have exceeded the WHO and CPCB standards in view of projected growth rates and industrial development. The air quality will further deteriorate both in area and magnitude. This will have serious consequences for the crop yield and food security.

A close review of the data analysis given in the ODA report which is an integration of almost 600 national and international papers and based on field studies shows that crop yield under air pollution stress is going to be reduced depending upon the geographical extent of the cultivated areas which is suffering from air pollution.Studies related to wheat, maize, rice and other crops indicate that crop damage is noticible within 6km radious of the location of air pollution on crop plants, which may extend over to 8-10 km radius from the point sources.

On the basis of available studies, SO_2 appears to be the most important air pollutant in relation to crop damage. In this connection, it may be pointed out that, CPCB has so far not prescribed any ambient standard for tropospheric Ozone. Moreover, data on Ozone are extremely limited, hence, the importance of Ozone in relation to crop yield can not be ascertained.

Air pollution monitoring presently is confined to major cities. Hence, an accurate profile of air pollution status in the rural and in agriculture areas is difficult to determine. However, the back ground level of air pollution in rural areas compiled from various sources indicate that ambient level of this pollutant sustain throughout the country.

The crop loss predicted for wheat, maize and rice are quite substantial. It may be seen that results of field and open top studies are quite close, though, not exactly comparable. At the same time values of crop yield losses in both cases are much higher as comparable to crop yield losses calculated on the basis of close top chamber fumigation studies.

It is assumed that 20% of the area under wheat cultivation has SO_2 levels of 6 mgm^{-3} i.e. 10% of the CPCB standards prescribed for rural areas, the wheat production is likely to suffer by 7.01% and for maize by 31.91% and for rice by 0.13% calculated on the assumptions stated above for wheat.

A broad assessment of the yield loss due to SO_2 for the following three cereal crops at 6mgm^{-3} of SO_2 (10% CPCB standard) calculated for 20% of the crop are as follows :

Wheat	0.70 million tones
Maize	0.50 million tones
Rice	0.02 million tones
Total	**1.22 million tones**

The above values are indication of crop losses but may not represent actual situation because the data underlining these estimation have a narrow base. In case of rice the values have been derived from the correlation between dose and yield characters. Thus, in strict sense it may not represent the actual crop losses. However, the results justify for taking up systematic field studies using open top chambers using filtered air for growing control plants. For other cereals, yield loss assessment is not feasible due to severe data constraints.

Data on pulses, vegetables, oil and fibre crops again reveal the negative impact of air pollution on crop performance. Direct yield measuring data though lacking, but the assessment of various morphohogical, physiological and biochemical parameters strongly argue that there is every reason to expect substantal reduction in the yield of these economically important agricultural crops. The loss of food grains results for greater consequences, in view of the food scarcity and rural economy. Moreover, it may also be emphasized that the constraint due to loss of food grains will become increasingly severe with the progressive growth of population, loss of crop area and increasing levels of air pollution. In addition, these losses are going to be recurring, hence, will seriously threaten the rural economy.

In case of vegetable crops the yield loss data does not gives an account of reduced consumer appeal, due to fading of the colour of vegetables or from changes in appearance which may make them less appealing to consumers.

Evidences from fumigation and field studies indicate that, air pollution would have an important effect on agricultural producation. Vulnerable crop areas such as, agricultural fields close to urban and peri-urban and industrial complexes are already suffering from the adverse impact of air pollution. This problem is likely to grow both in intensity and area in the coming years, in view of the projected demand for fossil fuels required to sustain, the desired high rate of economic growth. Perhaps the most significant aspect of the potential impact of growing air pollution on crop plants is that this will take place in the context of rapidly shrinking agriculture in the absolute terms as well as on per capita basis.

It is important to realize that the predictions on crop loss assessments are solely based on limited database and on fumigation experiments which have used, elevated concentrations of pollutants and performed in close top fumigation chambers or open top chambers. The duration of such experiments is necessarily restricted. Moreover, they have been performed under climate or growth conditions, which rarely corresponds to the climatic, or growth conditions of exposure of plants in field.

In addition, the review provides evidence to show that legal tolerance limits need to be reduced. Inspite of various limitations of data, these review emphasises the following aspects:

1. The air pollution is potential threat to crop yield.
2. The data clearly show that the present Ambient Air Quality standards prescribed by central pollution control Board (CPCB) are too high and they cannot protect crops from air pollution damage.
3. Inadequacy of our present knowledge about effect of air pollutants at the field levels, and
4. Lack of air quality data for rural/agricultural areas.

On the basis of data analysis given in the review some policy directions and future research priorities have been identified which are as under

1. Improved knowledge is needed on the effects of air pollutants on crop yield for different cultivars under various management practices in different agro-ecolo-gical zones.
2. An improved ability is required to 'scale-up' our under-standing of the effects of air pollution on crop yield.
3. An air quality monitoring network in rural/ agricultural areas is needed.
4. There is an urgent need to develop threshold concent-rations of crop damage and critical load for agricultural ecosystems in different agro-climatic regions.
5. Ambient air quality criteria for agricultural/rural areas need to be developed to protect crops from the growing threat of air pollution.

Ambient air quality has a significant localized impact and the percentage of population exposed is much higher in urban areas and in particular metropolitan cities. Therefore, since these areas have emerged as greatly stressed, the emphasis is on studying the causes for air pollution and interventions to ameliorate the condition in urban areas. Four reasons being - emissions from vehicles, thermal power plants, industries and refineries. The problem of indoor air pollution though an issue of concern in rural areas and urban slums has assumed significant attention lately.

Two major drawbacks in pollution control and prevention include:

* Unreliability of monitored and also submitted data.
* Inadequacy of competent and trained personnel in the regulatory agencies as also the enterprises calling for concerted effort at Capicity Building.

Economic Instruments for Air Environment Management

Emission reduction has to be the focus in India because of :

* High land to man ratio
* Low grade fuel mix
* Criticality of soil quality and water bodies in the economy of the country.

Strategies for emissions reducation essentially include Cleaner Fuels, Cleaner Technologies and Greener Growth

Economic Instruments are of three types:

* Fuel Taxes Covering Carbon Tax; Sulphur Tax and Ash Tax
* Emission Taxes and Emission Trading; and
* Taxes based on Material Intensity Per unit Service (MIPS) and Pollution Intensity Per Unit Service (PIPS).

Economic Instruments for Management of Ambient Air Quality (Point Sources)

A two pronged strategy is adopted.

Disperse and Dilute : Regional alliance for air quality management.

Increase in Sink Potential : Emission rights against creation of sinks, say, for GHGs.

Economic instruments are not yet in vogue because the regulatory mechanism is quite weak and ineffective.

How To Solve The Problem?

* Better information
* Consensus on issues and actions
* Political commitment & rigorous enforcement
* Identification of technical solution
* Economic analysis of options
* Appropriate macro-policy in place
* Institutional cooperation
* Private sector involvement
* Public participation
* Experiences from international experience

2

Beyond The Exhaust Emission Limits

Vinod S. Patel

The introduction of the exhaust emission control regualtions for passenger cars was introduced in the year 1970. Then Euro II standard was formed in 1996, which is still in effect, pollutants were sucessfully reduced by over 90%. Until Euro II, the EU had always based the increasingly restrictive pollutant limit values, possible deterioration of the vehicles emission perfor aree through a was in in the on technologcally feasible standards.

As a basis for a further reduction in exhaust emissions, the EU introduced the auto oil program. Based on values determined by the World Health Organization (WHO), it sets out air quality goals that shall be met in metropolitan areas beginning in 2010. Therefore, the auto oil program sets out the promise that further restrictions in exhaust emission limits should no longer be based on the technological feasibility but on the requirements for reaching air quality goals.

To reach these air quality goals, the EU passed directive 98/69/EC in 1998 to modify Directive 70/220/EEC. The new directive determines exhaust emission requirements for passenger and light commercial vehicles beginning in 2000 (Euro III) and 2005 (Euro IV). In addition to a restriction in exhaust emission values with separate proof of pollutant emissions for HC and NO_x, a changed driving cycle, a further exhaust emission test at low temperatures, on-board diagnostics (OBD) as well as regulations on recalls will be introduced. The OBD will alert the driver to a control panel. The driver can then immediately visit a manufacturer-authorized repair shop, and thereby contribute to operating the vehicle throughout its entire life span with as few emissions as possible.

In addition, OBD will also be used for exhaust emission tests (AU) beginning April 2002. For vehicles with catalytic converter, a reading of the OBD error log by a standardized and licensed scanning device will replace the previous control loop test.

The table below is taken from the directive text published in the Official Journal of the European Communities and illustrates the exhaust emission limits in effect for passenger cars (Vehicle class M1) and light commercial vehicles (Vehicle Class N1) for Euro III (row A-2000).

Table 1: Exhaust limits of Common pollutants for passenger cars

Year	Vechicle Class	Group	Refrence mass	Carbon monoxide mass		Hydro carbon mass carbons		Nitrogen oxide mass			Total mass ofhydro carbons and nitrogen oxides	Particle mass (1)
			Standard Value	CO L1		HC L2		Nox L3			HC+Nox L2+L3	PM L4
			Kg	g/km		g/km		g/km			g/km	g/km
			Gas	Diesel	Gas	Diesel	Gas	Diesel	Gas	Diesel	Diesel	
2000	M1 (2)	-	all	2,30	0,64	0,20	-	0,15	0,50	-	0,56	0,05
	N1 (3)	I	RW< 1305	2,30	0,64	0,20	-	0,15	0,50	-	0,56	0,05
		II	1305 <RW< 1760	4,17	0,80	0,25	-	0,18	0,65	-	0,72	0,07
		III	1760 <RW	5,22	0,95	0,29	-	0,21	0,78	-	0,86	0,10
	M1 (2)	-	all	1,00	0,50	0,10	-	0,08	0,25	-	0,30	0,025
	N1 (3)	I	RW< 1305	1,00	0,50	0,10	-	0,08	0,25	-	0,30	0,025
2005		II	1305 <RW< 1760	1,81	0,63	0,13	-	0,10	0,33	-	0,39	0,04
		III	1760 <RW	2,27	0,74	0,16	-	0,11	0,39	-	0,46	0,06

(1) Direct ignition engines.

(2) Exception: Vehicles with a maximum mass of more than 2.500 kg.

The overview below shows in simplified form the dates after which Euro III and Euro IV for passanger cars must be observed for first-time registration and EC type approval, and when vehicles must be equipped with OBD.

Initially, Euro I Euro II norms were scheduled to commence from April 2000 and April 2005 respectively. But on the recommendation of the Society of Indian Automobile Manufacturers (SIAM), they were proposed to June 99 and April 2000. It also considered SIAM's recommendation that stress should be laid on suitable norms that could bring down the increasing level of air pollution rather than on the technology applied for the purpose. The technology part could be left at the behest of the vehicle manufacturers.

Recently, SIAM has come out with a blueprint on the next stage of emission norms. The purpose is clear. SIAM has argued that the gap between the European and Indian stages of implementing the higher grades of pollution norms should be reduced. The Association feels that given the seriousness of the issue, it is better that this country too tries to address the problem in the shortest possible time frame, which is feasible.

According to the roadmap suggested by SIAM, the gap between European and Indian norms will be reduced from 13 years in 1991 to one year for passenger cars and two years for utility vehicles and commerical vehicles in meeting Euro IV equivalent norms which should be in place in Europe in 2006 for new type approval. Let's look at the details as has been listed in the table below :

Table 2 : Future norms proposal for passenger car segment

Norms	Europe Norms				SIAM recommendation
	New TA	All production	New TA	All production	Principal Parameters of fuel specific (EU)
Euro II		1996/1997		2000*	Petrol and Diesel Sulphur max: 0.05%
Euro III					Diesel : Sulphur ppm max 350
Euro IV					Petrol : Sulphur ppm max 50 Diesel : Sulphur ppm max 50

* NCR Other cities-six from date of notification

At present, the Euro II equivalent norms (called Bharat Stage II norms) have already been implemented in the National Capital Region of Delhi. The SIAM has suggested that these norms can be extended to six other cities provided petrol and diesel is available with 0.05% sulphur. However, according to some industry sources, this is not very likely to happen in 2004 year

For the multi-utility vehicle and commerical vehicle industry, SIAM has suggested the following time table.

Table 3 : Future norms proposal for Multi-utility Vehicel Segment

Norms level	Europe Norms				SIAM recommendation
	New TA	All Production	New TA	All Production	Principle Parameter of fuel specification (Per EU)
Euro II					
ClassI	1/1/97	1/198		1/4/02	Petrol and Diesel
Class II & III	1/10/97	1/10/98		1/4/02	Sulphur max - 0.05%
Euro III					
Class I	1/1/00	1/1/01	Skip		Petrol : Sulphur ppm max 150
Class II & III	1/1/01	1/1/02	Skip		Diesel : Sulphur ppm max 350
Euro IV					
Class I	1/1/05	1/106	1/4/07	1/4/08	Petrol : Sulphur ppm max 50
Class II & III	1/1/06	1/1/07	1/1/07	1/10/08	Diesel : Sulphur ppm max 50

* NCR : 1/04/2000/other cities: 1/10/2000

Table 4 : Future Norms Proposal for Commerical Vehicles Segment

Norms level	Europe Norms				SIAM recommendation
	New TA	All Production	New TA	All Production	Principal Parameters of fuel specification (per EU)
Euro II	1/10/95	1/10/96	1/4/02	1/4/03	Diesel : Sulphur max 0.05%
Euro III	1/10/00	1/10/01		Skip	Diesel : Sulphur max 350
Euro IV	1/10/05	1/10/06	1/10/07	1/10/08	Diesel : Sulphur max 50

Note : Light duty vehicels are classified as (for Euro III and Euro IV)

a. Class I- (rw less than equal to 1,305 kg)
b. Class II- (rw between 1,305 and 1,760 kg)
c. Class III- (rw greater than 1,760 kg)

One common factor seen from above tables, is the fact that SIAM has proposed skipping the Euro III norms for the utility vehicle and commercial vehicle industry. This suggestion is once again based on the premise of bridging the present gap between the European and Indian norms. Secondly, if these industries were to follow Euro III norms it would mean heavy investment in capital and new technology.

This investment would get only a short period of time for it to be amortized, which is not feasible given the low production volumes.

Table 5 : Progression of Euro norms for passanger cars in Europe (g/km)

Towards cleaner auto and fuel technologies in India: issues, recommendations, and manifesto for road map

Descrip-tion	Effective year of implementation		Carbon mono-	Hydro-carbon	Nitrogen oxides	Hydro-carbon+ nitrogen oxides	Particulate matter
	Euro	India					
Gasoline							
Euro I	1993	2000	2.72	-	-	0.97	-
Euro II	1996	2005	2.20	-	-	0.50	-
Euro III	2000	Not specified	2.20	0.20	0.15	-	-
Euro IV	2005	Not specified	1.00	0.10	0.08	-	-
Euro V[b]	2008	Not specified	0.04	0.05	0.04	Less then	0.015
Diesel							
Euro I	1993a	1996	2.72	-	-	0.97	0.14
Euro II	1996a	2000	1.06	-	0.566	0.71	0.080
Euro III	2000	Not specified	0.64	-	0.50	0.56	0.050
Euro IV	2005	Not specified	0.50	-	0.25	0.30	0.025
Euro V	2008	Not specified	0.45		0.20	0.20	0.015

a. For indirect and direct injection engines level of emission standards are different

b. Proposed will be drafted in year 2005

Note : Euro III and IV standards in Europe have not received final approval. The norms presented based on the proposal, which presently making the rounds in official European bodies.

Clean Cars Emission Standards

Table 6 : A Comparison of Emissions Standards

Pollutant	Clean Car Campaign SULEV Standard (grams/mile)	Current Federal Standard -Tier 1 (grams/mile)	Reduction (Percent)
Hydrocarbons (HC)	0.01	0.31	97%
Carbon Monoxide (CO)	1.0	4.2	76%
Nitrous Oxides (NOx)	0.02	0.6	97%
Particulate Matter (PM)	0.01	0.10	90%

Notes:

* Standards for light-duty trucks are less stringent in certain cases under Tier 1 standards. The same Clean Car Campaign-SULEV Standard applies to both passenger cars and light-trucks.
* Reductions based on a simple comparison of emission's standards for light duty automobiles SULEV standards are based on a120,000 mile lifetime instead of a 100,000 mile lifetime for Tier 1 standards.
* Achieving the full benefit of SULEV emission control technologies requires use of low-sulfur fuel, which is required in California but not yet available nationwide. Nevertheless, a vehicle that meets the SULEV standard will be cleaner than an average vehicle. Since most vehicles stay on the road for many years, its emissions performance will improve as low-sulfur fuel is phased in, starting from 2004 under the new fuel quality standards that EPA has proposed under Tier 2.

Sources

1. Cayot J. 1999. Pollution from thermal engine passenger cars in urban areas. Paris: Federation Des Industries Des Equipments Des Vehicle (FIEV).
2. Khadilkar R. B. Basu S. and Kumar R.R. 1999. New engine-semission and norms: an overview. Pune: Tata Enginering and Locomotive Company Limited.
3. Bhatnagar A.K. and Raje N.R. 1999. Fuel quality aspects related to auto emissions and challenges ahead. Faridabad Research and Development Centre, Indian Oil Corporation Limited.

3

Urban Air Pollution : Sources and Effects

H.V. Bhavnani

Sources of Air Pollution:

A) The combustion of gasoline and other hydrorcarbon fuels in automobiles, trucks, and jet airplanes produces several primary pollutants; nitrogen oxides, gaseous hydrocarbons, and carbon monoxide, as well as large quantities of particulates, chiefly lead.

In the presence of sunlight, nitrogen oxides combine with hydrocarbons to form a secondary class of pollutants, the photochemical oxidants, ozone and the eye-stinging peroxyacetylnitrate (PAN). Nitrogen oxides also react with oxygen in the air to form nitrogen dioxide, a foul-smelling brown gas.

In urban areas where transporation is the main cause of air pollution, nitrogen dioxide tints the air, blending with other contaminats and the atmospheric water vapour to produce brown smog. Although the use of catalytic converters has reduced smog-producing compounds into production of nitrous oxide, which contributes substantially in global warming.

B) Burning of fossil fuels (oil and coal) in generating stations, factories, office buildings, and homes and by the incineration of garbage. The massive combustion produces tons of ash, soot, and other particulates, responsible for the gray smog of cities along with enormous quantities of sulfur oxides. These oxides rust iron, damage building stone, decompose nylon, tarnish silver, and kill plants. Air pollution from cities also affects rural areas for many miles downwind.

Industrial process exhibits its own pattern of air pollution. Petroleum refinereis are responsible for extensive hydrocarbon and particulate pollution. Iron and steel mills, metal smelters, pulp and paper mills, chemical plants, cement and asphalt plants-all discharge vast amounts of various particulates. Un insulated high-voltage power lines ionize the adjacent air, forming ozone and other hazardous pollutants.

Airborne pollutants from other sources include insecticides, herbicides, radioactive fallout, and dust from fertilizers, mining operations, and livestock feedlots.

The air pollutants originate from fixed sources and mobile sources.

Fixed Sources:

Fixed air pollution sources include those sources which are located in one place which include industries

Industries are major producers of carbon monoxide (CO), carbon dioxide (CO_2), Sulfur dioxide (SO_2), NOx particulates, and other air toxins.

Mobile Sources:

Mobile air pollution sources include those sources which are free to move from one area to another. Hence, mobile sources have the potential to pollute any area they visit.

Air pollution from mobile sources is almost solely based on the automobile and transportation of fuels and chemicals through tankers.

TYPES OF AIR POLLUTANTS

I) Particulate Pollutants:

Particulate Matter

Tiny solid particles, such as dust, smoke, and exhaust

fumes, which are released into the air and create pollution. Particulate matter pollutants originate from automobile exhaust and industrial processes.

Particles are present everywhere, but high concentrations or specific types of particles have been found to pose a serious danger to human health.

"Particulate matter is a combination of fine solids such as dirt, soil dust, pollens, molds, ashes, and soot; and aerosols that are formed in the atmosphere from gaseous combustion by-products such as volatile organic compounds and agricultural activities.

II) Gaseous Pollutants:

1. Carbon Monoxide (CO)

Gaseous particles resulting from the combustion of fossil fuels and automobile exhaust. Some carbon monoxide sources are oxidized to carbon dioxide.

Carbon monoxide is a colourless, odorless gas.

2. Sulfur Dioxide (SO_2)

Gaseous particles resulting from burning of fossil fuels, particularly by heat and power generation facilities, and volcanic gases. Sulfur dioxide has a very pungent odour. Sulfur dioxide is formed when sulfur compounds react with oxygen during combustion.

3. Nitrogen Compounds (NOx):

Nitrogen compounds are gaseous sources of air pollution, generated through automobile exhaust, fertilizer plants, and the burning of fossil fuels. Nitrogen compounds are broken down to primary and secondary pollutants.

Primary pollutants include NO, NH_3, and NOx compounds which are formed from a combination of NO with NO_2. Secondary pollutants include NO_2, HNO_3 and MNO_3.

4. Air Toxins

This category describes a mix of air pollution sources, including metals (Hg, Pb, Zn), organic sources (Various solvents), acids (H_2SO_4), and radioactive substances (1-131, BA-140, Zr-95).

EFFECTS OF AIR POLLUTION

I) Particulate Pollutants and its Effects:

Particles of special concern to the protection of lung health are those known as 'fine particles' These are less than 2.5 microns in diameter (for comparison, a human hair is about 75 microns in diameter).

Fine particles are easily inhaled deeply into the lungs, where they can be absorbed into the blood stream or remain embedded for long periods of time. "A recent study showed a 17 percent increase in mortality risk" in areas with higher concentrations of small particles.

Particulate matter air pollution is especially harmful to people with lung diseases such as asthma and chronic obstructive pulmonary disease (COPD), which includes chronic bronchitis and emphysema, as well as people with heart disease.

Exposure to particulate air pollution can trigger asthma attacks and cause wheezing, coughing and respiratory irritation in individuals with sensitive airways.

Recent research has also linked exposure to relatively low concentrations of particulate matter with premature death. Those at greatest risk are the elderly and those with preexisting respiratory or heart diseases.

II) Gaseous Pollutants and its Effects :

1. Carbon monoxide accumulates in indoor air, it can cause headache, dizziness, nausea, fatigue, excessive yawning, decreased hearing, heart palpitasions, loss of appetite, and vomiting. The symptoms are frequently similar to influenza symptoms. Older people, pregnant women, and people with a history of heart disease are particularly sensitive to cause collapse, unconsciousness and in extreme cases, death.
2. Nitrogen dioxide can cause eye, nose, throat and respiratory tract irritation. Prolonged exposure has been shown

to lower resistance to respiratory infection and can be damaging to respiratory tissue.

3. Sulfur dioxide is particularly threatening to people with asthma, in whom it can constrict the airways leading to and from the lungs, making breathing difficult. People with lung disease and allergies may also have adverse reactions to sulfur dioxide fumes. Sulfur dioxide can also cause irritation of skin and eyes.

4. Oxides of nitrogen-NOx causes a wide variety of health and environmental impacts because of various compounds and derivatives in the family of nitrogen oxides, including nitrogen dioxide, nitric acid, nitrous oxide, nitrates, and nitric oxide.

* **Ozone (Smog)**—is formed when NOx and volatile organic compounds react in the presence of heat and sunlight. Children, people with lung diseases such as asthma, and people who work or exercise outside are susceptible to adverse effects such as damage to lung tissue and damaged vegetation and reduced crop yields.

* **Acid Rain**—NOx and sulfur dioxide react with other substances in the air to form acids which fall to earth as rain, fog, snow or dry particles. Some may be carried by wind for hundreds of miles. Acid rain damages; causes deterioration of cars, buildings and historical monuments; and cause lakes and streams to become acidic and unsuitable for many fish.

* **Particles**—NOx reacts with ammonia, moisture, and other compounds to form nitric acid and related particles. Human health concerns include effects on breathing and the respiratory system, damage to lung tissue, and premature death. Small particles penetrate deeply into sensitive parts of the lungs and can cause or worsen respirtory disease such as emphysema and bronchitis, and aggravate existing heart disease.

* **Water Quality Deterioration**—Increased Nitrogen load-

ing in water bodies, particularly coastal estuaries, upsets the chemical balance of nutrients used by aquatic plants and animals. Additional nitrogen accelerates "eutrophication", which leads to oxygen depletion and reduces fish and shellfish populations.

* **Global Warming**—One member of the NOx, nitrous oxide, is a greenhouse gas. It accumulates in the atmosphere with other greenhouse gasses causing a gradual rise in the earth's temperature. This will lead to increased risks to human health, a rise in the sea level and other adverse changes to plant and animal habitat.

* **Toxic Chemicals**—In the air, NOx reacts readily with common organic chemicals and even ozone, to form a wide variety of toxic products, some of which may cause biological mutations.

* **Visibility Impairment**—Nitrate particles and nitrogen dioxide can block the transmission of light, reducing visibility in urban areas and on a regional scale in our nationai parks.

4

Aerodynamics of Vehicle For Reduced Air pollution

G. Raja, M. Subramanian and K. Balagurunathan

In recent years concern over the contribution of diesel engine vehicle in particulate emissions - Suspended Particulate Matter (SPM), Respiratory Dust Particles (RDP) and Oxides of Nitrogen (NOx) in environmental Pollution has resulted in significant increase in research and regulatory activity world-wide.

Aerodynamics makes its major impact on modern cars and trucks through its contribution to "road load". The aerodynamics shape influences the positive pressure on front of the vehicle and negative pressure on the rear of the vehicle. The negative pressure on the rear of the vehicle makes the dust particulates to follow the vehicle. This dust get deposited on the vehicle back as well as on the people following the vehicle. This is very high when the vehicle is moving with very high speed. The aerodynamic design helps to reduce the positive pressure at the front reducing the drag. The negative pressure which influences the dust particles follow behind the vehicle.

Introduction

Apart from the engine particulate matter from C.I. Engine (0.5 g/m^3) and S.I. Engines (0.1g/m^3). The dust particles in and around the atmosphere get collected and deposited on the vehicle back and the people. The lay out of exhaust system in vehicle and its body shape at the back of the vehicle play an important role in respiratory dust particles deposit.

By properly modifying different of the vehicle the aerodynamic drag can be reduced their by resistance to vehicle movement is reduced and better fuel economy can be achieved.

Mechanics Of Air Flow Around A Vehicle :—

The gross flow over the body of a car is governed by relationship between velocity and pressure expressed in Bernoulli's equation. (Bernoulli's equation assumes incompressible flow, which is reasonable for automotive aerodynamics, whereas the equivalent relationship for compressible flow is the Euler equation.) The equations:

Pastatics + dynamics = Potal.

$P_s + 1/2\ Pv^2 = Pt$

Where : P = Density of air,

v= Velocity of air (relative to the car)

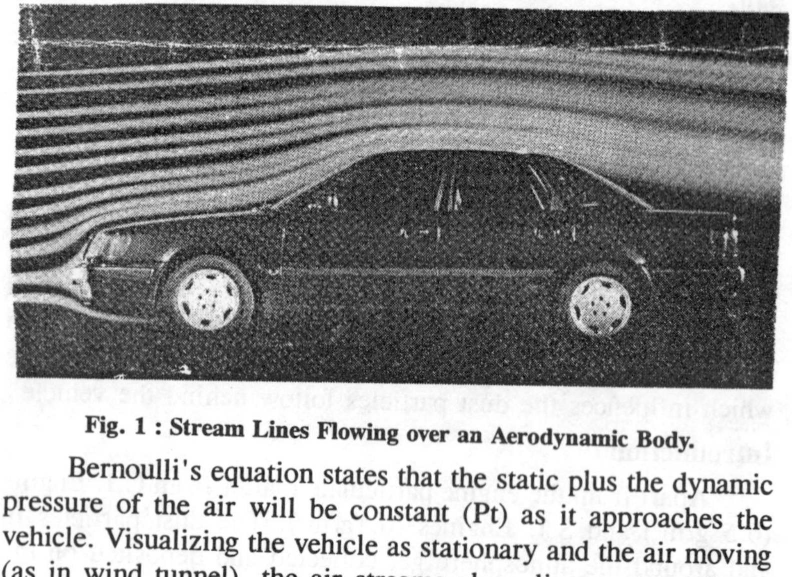

Fig. 1 : Stream Lines Flowing over an Aerodynamic Body.

Bernoulli's equation states that the static plus the dynamic pressure of the air will be constant (Pt) as it approaches the vehicle. Visualizing the vehicle as stationary and the air moving (as in wind tunnel), the air streams along lines, appropriately called "stream lines". A bundle of streamlines froms a stream tube. The smoke streams used in a wind tunnel allow stream tubes to be visualized as illustrated in figure (1).

At a distance from the vehicle the static pressure is simply the ambient, or barometric pressure (Patm). The dynamic pressure is produced by the relative velocity, which is constant for all streamlines approaching the vehicle. Thus the total pressure P_t, is the same for all streamlins and is equal to $P_s + 1/2pv^2$.

Vehicle, and others below, by inference, on streamline must go straight to the body and stagnate (the one shown impinging on the bumper of the car). At that point the relative velocity has gone to zero. With the velocity term zero, the static pressure observed at that point on the vehicle will be p_t. That is, if a pressure tap is placed on the vehicle at this point, it will record the total pressure.

Consider what must happen to the streamlines flowing above the hood. As they first turn in the upward direction, the curvature is concave upward. At a distance well above the vehicle where the streamlines are still straight, the static pressure must be same as the ambient. In order for the air stream to be curved upward, the static pressure in that region must be higher than ambient to provide the force necessary to turn the air flow. If the static pressure is higher, then the velocity must decrease in this region in order to obey Bernoulli's equation.

Conversely, as the flow turns to follow the hood (downward curvature at the lip of the hood) the pressure must go below ambient in order to bend the flow, and the velocity must increase.

Pressure Distribution on a Vehicle :

Figure (2) shows experimentally measured Pressures plotted Perpendicular to the Surface. The pressures are indicated as being negative or positive with respect to the ambient pressure measured some distance from the vehicle.

Note that negative pressure is developed at the front edge of the hood as the flow rising over the front of the vehicle attempts to turn and follow horizontally along the hood. The adverse pressure gradient in this region has the potential to stall the boundary layer flow creating drag in this area. In recent years, styling detail in front hood line has given high priority to avoid separation on the hood and the drag penalty that results.

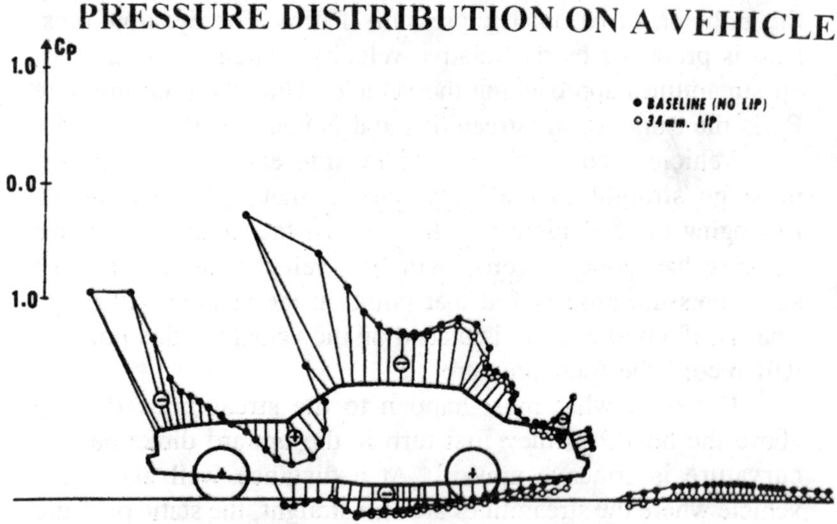

Fig. 2 : Pressure Coefficient Plotted Normal to Surface.

Near the base of the windshield and cowl, the flow must be turned upward, thus high pressure is experienced. The high Pressure region is an ideal location for inducting air for climate control systems, or engine intake and has been used for this purpose in countless vehicles in the past. The high pressure are accompained by lower velocities in this region, which is an aid to keeping the wind shield wipers from being disturbed by aerodynamics forces.

Over the roof line the pressure again goes negative as the airflow tries to follow the contour. Evidence of the low pressure in this region is seen in the billowing action of the fabric roof on convertibles. The pressure remains low down over the backlite and on to the trunk because of the continuing curvature. It is in this area that flow separation is most likely. Design of the angles and details of the body contour in this region require critical concern for aerodynamics. Because of the low pressure, the flow along the sides of the car will also attempt to feed air into this region and may add to the potential for separation. The flow along the sides is drawn up into the low-pressure region in the rear area, combining the flow over the roof to form vortices trailing off the back of the vehicle.

The choice of the backlite angles and deck lid lengths on the back of a car as a direct impact on aerodynamic forces through control of the separation point. Separation must occur at some point, and the smaller the area, generally the lower the drag. Theoretically, the ideal form of an aerodynamic viewpoint is teardrop rear shape. That is a conical shape that tapers off to a point with shallow angles of 15 degrees or less. It was recognized as early as the 1930s that because the area toward the point of the cone is quite small, the end of the ideal vehicle can be cut off without penalty of a large separation area. The blunt rear end shape allows greater head in the back seat without substantially increasing drag. This characteristic shape as acquired the name "Kamm-back" deposition on the backlite and taillights. The high degree of turbulence in the seperation zone entrains moisture and dirt picked up from the roadway by the tires. If the seperation zone includes these items, dirt will be depoisted on this area and vision will be obstructed. Figure (3) illustrates this phenomenon.

Whether sepration will occur at the rear edge of the roofline is strongly dependent on the shape at the location and the backlite angles. For the vehicle on the left, the sharp edge at the roofine promotes separation at this point. While a well defined separation boundary helps minimize aerodynamic buffeting, the inclusion of the backlite in the separation area promotes dirt deposition on the window.

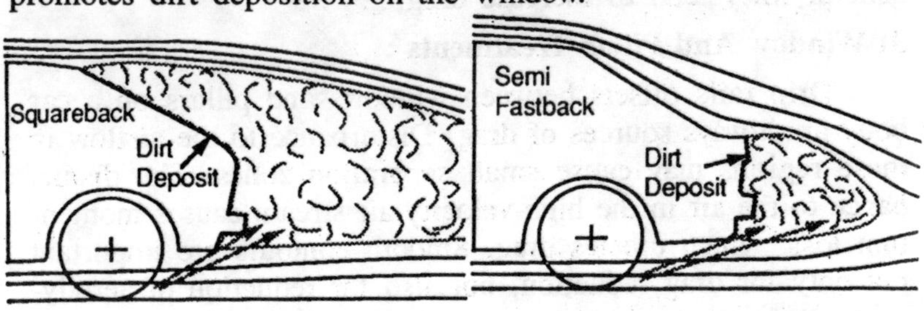

Fig. 3 : Effect of Seperation Point on Dirt Deposition.

Although the vehicle on the right has a comparable bake-lite angles, the smooth transition at the rear of the roof and the addition of a modest trunk extension encourages the air streams to follow the vehicle contours at the end of the deck, helping to stabilize the separation zone and minimize buffering. Only the tail light region is exposed to road dirt with this design.

AERODYNAMIC AIDS

1) Bumper Spoilers :

Front bumper spoilers are aerodynamic surfaces extending downward from the bumper to block and redirect the shear flow that impact on the underbody components. While the spoiler contributes pressure drag, atleast with a shallow depth the reduction in underbody drag is more significant. As spoiler depth is increased, eventually the increased pressure drag outweighs further, reduction in underbody drag and the overall drag increases.

Air dams are flow-blocking surfaces installed at the premier of the radiator to improve flow through the radiator at lower vehicle speeds. The improvement derives from the decreased pressure behind the radiator fan, and may reduce drag by reudction of pressure on the firewall.

2) Decklid Spoilers :

Spoilers and air fans on the rear deck may serve several purposes. By deflecting the air upward, as shown in figure (4) the pressure is increased on the rear deck creating a down force at the most advantageous stabilize the vortices in the separation flow, this reduces aerodynamic buffering. In general, they tend to increase drag.

3) Window And Pillar Treatments :

Drip rails offsets between windows and pillars on a car body are always sources of drag. Disturbance to the airflow in these regions may cause small separation zones. The disturbance to the air in the high-velocity air stream causes momentum loss, which creates drag. Smooth contours are important not only for drag reduction, but also for reduction of aerodynamic noise.

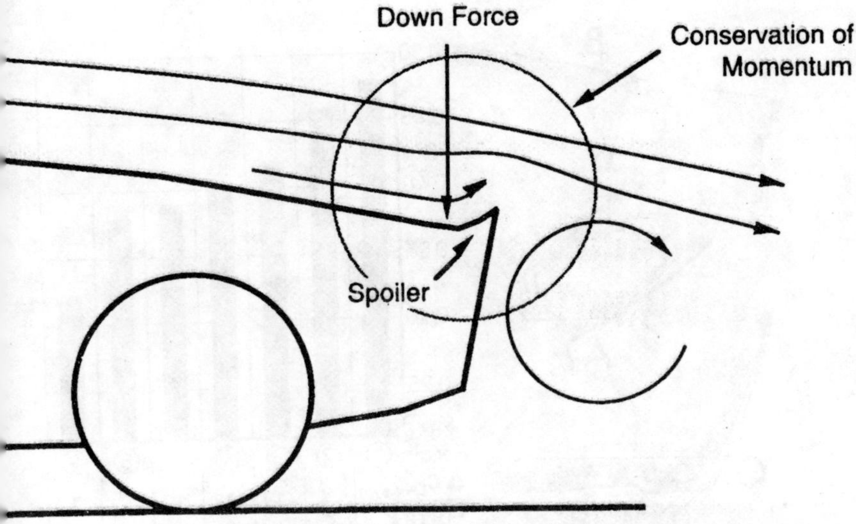

Fig. 4 : Influence of a Spoiler on flow over the Rear.

The optimization is founded on the premise that the styling concept of the car is established and aerodynamic improvement can only be attempted in the form of charges to detail in the styling. An example of the optimization is shown in figure (5). The sketches show minor modifications in detail such as a change in the air dam (H), hood line (B), A-pillar shape (C) and D-Pillar shape (D and E). The graph illustrates the magnitude of drag reduction obtained from various combinations of these changes. The power of drag reduction by attention to details is illustrated by the fact that an overall drag reduction of 21% is achieved. This reduction in drag improves fuel economy of the vehicle.

Exhaust System Pipe layout in a Vehicle :

The exhaust gases emitted from the engine should be properly routed in the vehicle so that the dust particles and particulate matter fall on the road. This will reduce the dust particles directed towards a person, which cause cancer effect.

Conclusion

By proper vehicle shape, the air flowing around the

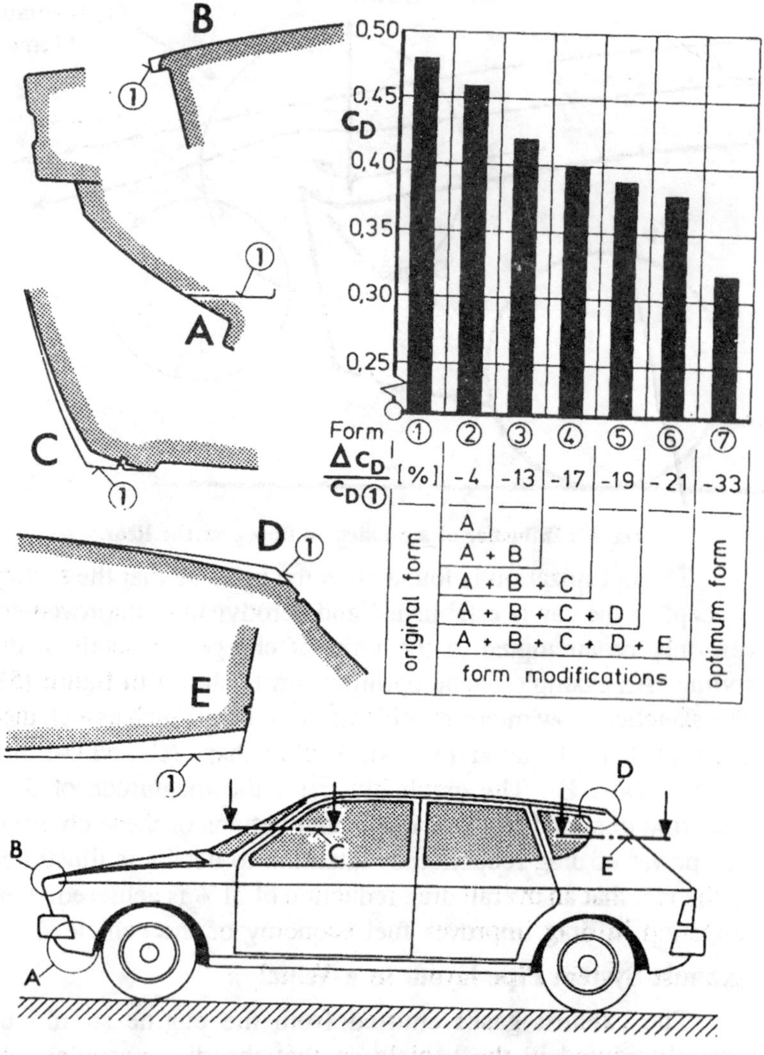

Fig. 5 : Optimization of Body Detail.

vehicle can be steamlined, by this way dust particles picked by vehicles can be reduced.

By directing exhaust gas tail pipe towards ground, the smoke effect can be reduced on the roadways.

Fig. 6 : Exhaust System of the Engine.

REFERENCES

1. Powloski. J Body Engineering, Business books Ltd., 1969.
2. Thomas D. Gillespi., Vehicle e Foundamentals of Vehicle Dynamics, Society of Automotive Engineers, Inc. 400 Commonwealth Drive Warrendale.

5

Eco-Friendly Lighting Design Options for Controlling Air Pollution

Neena Jaju

Coal is a major electrical energy source in India. Increased coal consumption over the past four decades has led to nine-fold increase in energy related carbon emissions in the atomsphere. Artifical lighting in residential and commerical spaces is a major and conspicuous consumption of electrical energy; and thus constit-utes an appropriate target for energy conservation efforts. Today, lighting alone accounts for about 17 per cent of the country's total electricity consumption. An average house-hold dedicates 5 to 10 per cent of its energy budget to lighting, while commercial establishments consume 20-30 per cent of their total energy just for lighting. Such a high lighting load needs to be addressed in relation to the technologies developed during the past 10 years, that can help to cut the lighting costs by 30 to 60 per cent, while enhancing lighting quality and reducing environmental impacts. The present paper focuses upon the eco-friendly lighting technology and design options available in reducing air pollution caused by the electricity generating stations emitting enormous amount of carbon dioxide and sulphur dioxide. The various related aspects like lighting and lighting maintenance have been brought forth. The paper, in addition, discusses the far reaching implications of energy sensitive lighting design and the strategies for removing market barries to make energy efficent lighting products available and affordable to the end users.

The global climatic changes are primarily due to the burning of fossil fuels and the resulting build up of carbon dioxide and other "green house gases" in the atmosphere. India's energy-related carbon emissions have grown nine-fold over the past four decades with 243.3 million metric tonnes of carbon released from the consumption and flaring of fossil fuels in 1999. India ranked fifth in the world behind the United States, China, Russia and Japan. India's contribution to world carbon emissions is expected to increase in coming years, with an estimated average growth rate of 3.2 per cent. India's reliance on low-quality coal with a high carbon content is the primary impetus for this expected increase. About 70 per cent of electricity come from coal and 64 per cent of all carbon emissions come from coal (Energy Information Administration, 2001). Further, according to Bhattacharya and Mitra (1998) electricity generated from 81 major coal fired thermal power plants in India results in 1.1 thousand tonnes of CO_2 emissions, 7.6 thousand tonnes of SO_2 emissions and 1.1 thousand tonnes of NOx emission per day.

Artificial lighting accounts for 17 per cent of all electricity consumed in India. An average household dedicates 5 to 10 per cent of its energy budget to lighting, while commercial establishments consume 20 to 30 per cent of this total energy just for lighting, becoming a conspicuous consumer of electrical energy; and thus constituting an appropriate target for energy conservation efforts. Lighting designers and consultants have a great opportunity to contribute to a significantly cleaner environment. Infact, such alarming figures on air pollution creates the responsibility to design lighting system that are more than aesthetically pleasing. Every energy reducing component within our technological grasp should be employed to ensure that every lighting project is energy sensitive. The present paper focuses upon the eco-friendly lighting technology and design options available to control air pollution. In a typical residential or commerical lighting installation, where 40 to 50 per cent of energy is wasted by obsolete equipments, inadequate maintenance, or inefficient use; the options discussed herewith can provide long term solution to the environmental issues.

1. New Design Criteria

Improving upon the design strategies both with regard to the lighting system and the visual task play a critical role to increase energy efficiency of lighting. One of the most important considerations in lighting system design is the specification of the required illuminance level. The magnitude of this level and the method by which it is achieved strongly influence the electrical power input (Kilowatts) needed to operate the system. Of equal importance is lighting quality, to which a number of separate factors contribute: visibility, discomfort glare, surface brightness ratios, the directional flow of light for revealing human facial features and the textured surfaces of the building interior.

Increased knowledge of the relationship between visibility and illuminance has led to develop new methods of lighting design and designing of visual tasks with the more meaningful approach visibility is the new design tool. Not only it is a most useful measure of lighting quality, but through visual performance studies, it can also be used for specifying lighting levels in numerous working environments. The light-reflecting properties of an object and the direction of the incident light striking it have a greater effect on visibility than level of illuminance itself. Thus, the traditional provision of a uniform illuminance level in the entire working space is being replaced by controlled illuminance concentrated at the work station. If work locations are uncertain or flexible within a space, then a general lighting scheme can be employed using luminaries with specific intensity distribu-tions in computer-designed layouts. This can provide a uniform level of visibility but a non-uniform illuminance level across the interior space. Task lighting integrated into office furniture has recently found wide acceptance. Here, the artificial illumination is confirmed to the work station. By providing good visibility where it is required, the available light is used most economically and effectively.

The design of the visual task itself can work significantly towards reducing the lighting load. Understanding the principles of visibility design like contrast, veiling reflections and equivalent sphere illumination can enable to plan visual tasks for optimum results.

i. Contrast, and the eye's sensitivity to it, is the most important parameter in describing visibility. For an object to be perceived clearly there must be an appropriate luminance difference / contrast between the task detail and its immediate background. Size, colour and the time available to see the task may also be used to describe a visual task.

ii. Veiling reflections are one of the most important factors affecting lighting quality; a non-uniform luminance distribution surrounding the visual task is another, but less significant. Veiling reflections are specular reflections superimposed upon diffuse reflections from an object that partially or totally obscure visual details by reducing luminance contrast and therefore visibility. Veiling reflections may be minimized by positioning over head luminaries (or employing ones with appropriate intensity distributions) in such a way that most of the light passes in front of and across the observer, perpendicular to the direction in which he faces, so minimizing specular reflections in the direction of view. This can also be achieved by employing multi-layered polari-zing panels in luminaries that produce vertically polarized light.

iii. Equivalent sphere illumination (ESI) quantifies the effects of veiling reflections and other factors that affect lighting quality and is therefore, an appropriate design parameter. Expressed in units of foot-candles or lux, ESI is a measure of visibility. It is the level of illuminance under reference lighting conditions that will provide the same task visibility as the particular lighting conditions of interest. Reference lighting conditions are those produced in a photometric sphere, which gives a perfectly diffuse illuminance and in which internal luminances are equal from point to point sphere illumination produces very few veiling reflections, but it is not necessarily the optimum for good in the same glass reflector lamps as incandesent lamps and the ESI concept can and thus help designers to prodnce good quality lighting and reduce lighting energy consumption, encouraging them to design for visibility and avoid unnecessary high illuminance levels in non-working areas.

2. Energy Efficient Lamps/Luminaries

Lighting technology has evolved in recent years and much has been learnt in the recent years. Advances in lamp and luminarie design has created a revolution in the field of lighting. Improved designs of both incandescent and fluorescent fixtures have been developed with energy- efficient component been incorporated into them. In office buildings, the typical fluorescent fixture with two 4-feet fluorescent lamps with magnetic ballasts uses 90 to 100 watts of power. However, new fixtures with special thin-diameter lamps that use better electrodes and coatings than do the older ones and with electronic ballasts consume about 60 watts; producing about the same lumen output. Improved variety in fluorescent ballasts could be another consideration to fulfill one's energy saving goals. The improved electromag-netic ballasts and electronic ballasts raise the efficiency of the fixtures by 12 to 30 per cent. The new electro magnetic ballasts reduce ballast losses, fixture temperature, and system wattage; and since they operate at cooler temperatures, they last longer than the older ones. Electronic ballasts operate at very high frequency that eliminates flickers and noise, and are even more efficient than the improved electromagnetic ballasts. Further, energy savings are possible through use of fixtures with improved designs with special energy- efficient light control components like reflectors, refractors, diffusers, lovers and baffles. These light control components pro-vide for better reflecting geometry and can be installed to optimize light distribution for the reduced number of lamps.

Another significant revolution is the development of compact fluorescent lamp. A CFL can replace incandescent lamp that is about 3 to 4 times its wattage, saving upto 75 per cent of the initial lighting energy. An 18 watt CFL can be substituted with a 75 watt standard incandescent lamp. Replacement of a standard incandescent lamp with a CFL of similar lumen output can keep half ton of carbon dioxide out of earth's atmosphere (Vera, 1992). CFLs are also packaged ans can be successfully used in recessed fixtures as ellipsidal refletors (type—ER) also, reflector or parabolic refle-ctor FLs can be utilized for the purpose of flood and spot lighting. These new CFL fixtures with built-in electronic ballasts and polished metal reflectors have high energy saving value. Although CFLs cost about 10 to 20 times more than comparable incandescent bulbs, they last 10 to 15 times as long. This energy saving characteristic and superior longevity make CFLs one of the best energy-efficient investments for residential and commercial buildings (Jaju and George, 2001).

Further, halogen lamps have also evolved as reasonably effective substitute for incandescent lamps, specifically, where dimming capabilities are needed, where colour rendering is critical, and where operating hours are short. For example, halogen lamps can be used to spot light, art work, retail items, and conference areas or meeting rooms as well as to provide mood lighting in restaurants. In stores, most of the displays are lit by incandescent spotlight, typically using 150 watts per lamp, which may not be the best type of lamp for their application. This can successfully be substitued by a 60 watt special halogen IR lamps, which not only reduce energy waste but also enhance the quality of light.

3. Energy Management Lighting Control Systems

Lighting controls are devices for turning light on and off or for dimming them. They include switches, dimmers, timers, motion detectors and photosensor. In most applications, proper use of controls provide a great opportunity to avoid waste of lighting energy by reducing the light sources on-time. Energy can be saved by turning off or dimming lamps. Controls make this energy savings more convenient and predictable (Leslie and Conway, 1996).

i. Switches are manual controls that turn lamps on and off. To avoid wastage of energy, people must use switches to turn off lamps when the space is unoccupied or light is not needed. Locating switches in convenient locations make people more likely to run off lamps when not needed. Adding additional switches in numerous convenient points for shared space having multiple entrances makes it easier for people to turn off lights in unused areas. Also, a "switch sticker" is a simple message affixed to a switches plate to remind residents to save energy, and as easy way to encourage them to develop energy conserving behaviours.

ii. Dimmers are used to vary the light output of lamps, and are used in rooms where a range of light output is desirable. Operating lamps at less than full output saves energy. Dimming incandescent or fluorescent lamps decreases light output and energy use. A simple replacement of a switch with a dimmer would save energy by dimming incandescent lamps. However, dimming incandescent lamps reduces their lumen output more than their wattage, making them inefficient as they are dimmed. In case of fluorescent lamps, both magnetic and electronic ballasts are available with dimming capabilities. Electronic ballasts offer quieter operation, dimming over a wider range, and greater energy savings.

iii. Timers turn lamps on , either manually or automatically, after a designed time period.Three types of timers for lighting are interval timers, plug-located timers, and socket-located timers. Interval timers save energy and may extend the service life of lamps by turning off when light is not largely needed. Plug-located timers are used for security, when the home is not occupied for an extended period of time, wherein operating low-wattage and / or fluorescent lamps save energy. Socket-located timers are used on luminaries that have incandescent lamps and are used in spaces occupied for short periods of time such as closets or pantries, where the lamps are likely to be left on.

iv. Motion detectors, often called occupancy sensors, automatically turn lamps on when motion is detected and off when no motion is detected. There are two primary types of motion detectors, infra red and ultrasonic. Infrared sensors respond to a change in infrared heat motion in a space, and ultrasonic sensors respond to a change in ultrasonic frequencies caused by motion in the space, Motion detectors save energy and can extend the service life of lamps by automatically turning lamps off, when a room is unoccupied.

v. Photosensors are light detecting devices that operate the lamp when the surrounding light drops below a specified level. Advance designs gradually raise or lower the fluorescent/ incandescent light levels with changing daylight levels. A photosensor can be integrated into a night light to automatically switch off the night light in the morning. Photosensor can also be used in an interior space wherein daylight is available in varying intensities throughout the day. The photo-device turns the electric light according to the available daylight, maintaining the consistency in the light level in the room; thereby saving the extra watt.

4. Daylighting

Since the energy crisis of the 1970s, daylighting has received attention as an energy saving design strategy for buildings. The benefits of daylighting include energy savings, power failure tolerance, and productivity. For most climates and many building types day lighting can save energy. A typical office building can reduce its energy consumption up to 20 per cent by using daylighting (Lesile, 1994). Daylighting in air-conditioned buildings is particularly important as the heat component of artificial lighting, is more than that of natural light. For removing every extra watt of heat energy from artificial lighting, one-third watt of energy is consumed in the air-conditioning plant (Gupta, 1992). However, environmental constants set up by the structure and size of the building envelope and the variability of daylight pose crucial challenges that refer specifically to daylighting. These include creating acceptable illumination gradient; minimizing direct glare, excessive brightness ratios and veiling reflections; diffusing the light by means of multiple reflections; and using the full aesthetic potential of daylighting.

Numerous techniques and design strategies are available that can address these challenges to a great extent and it is worthwhile to address these strategies in the schematic design process of any building. The orientaion and form of the building are critical to successful daylighting scheme. It is not only the external form, but also the shape of internal spaces that must be considered. The window geometry constitutes an important component in any daylighting strategies. Height and placement of windows, window treatments that can effectively filter and diffuse direct sun light, are aspects that need to worked upon.

Also, choosing the right window glazing material is critical to successful daylighting design. Glazing comes in a variety of types: clear, tinted, heat absorbing, reflective and selectively reflective. Slection of these would depend upon the amount of daylight and solar heating desired. Further, light shelves/ outdoor lowver system/indoor venetian blinds are very effective in redirecting light up to the ceiling controlling glare and limiting the collection of light. Use of skylight, clerestory and monitory in buildings are also options for optimally utilizing daylight. The spacing, placement, use of slope, splayed openings, shades and reflections, interior reflectors, heliostat-mounted reflectors etc. are crucial to the design of skylights. In case of clerestories and monitors, their orientation, use of sun catcher baffles, overhang and diffusing baffles, light scoops etc. are essential components (Lechner, 1991).

Alternatively, there are other emerging techologies such as switchable building skins and beam daylighting that provide the worker the ability to choose variations of his own light environment. Switchable building skins allow repositioning of apertures, redirection of sunlight, and patterning of view and light. Bean daylighting technologies can bring sunlight to remote work spaces and can also direct sunlight to exterior spaces facades. As we understand more about the holistic effects of light, these developing technologies may take on greater significance in the design of our environments (Leslie, 1991).

5. Solar lighting

Photo-volataic equipments have potentials to offer substantial quality of life emprovements as well as energy and cost savings. PV lighting systems are after the least cost method of household lighting and electricity. Rural households that currently use kerosene Lamps for light comprise the principal market for PV. lighting systems, and for an increasing segment of these house holds, PV systems are affordable. For home lighting, the cost of an PV lighting system is comparable to a family's average monthly expenditure for candles, kerosene or dry cell batteries. PV systems produce electric power with no CO_2 emissions. Annual CO_2 emission from kerosene lighting in most rural households averages around 0.3 tonnes of CO_2 per house hold, or some 300 tonnes of CO_2 per 1000 household per year. Therefore, the carbon emission offset is calculated at axproximately 6 tonnes of CO_2 over the 20-year life on PV system. For 1000 homes with PV lighting systems, atleast 6000 tonnes CO_2 will be displaced. Displacing the power grid avoids additional potential carbon emission (Plas, 1998).

However, at the same time it is crucial to understand that the success of PV lighting systems's implementation has been greatly determined by quality of the components (solar modules, battery, charge controller, compact or tubular fluorescent lamps, wiring and mounting). Therefore regular testing of PV lighting systems for electronic efficiency, charge-discharge eficiency, light output, reliability, protections, temperature compensation etc. need to be carried out for effective results. If a well-designed PV lighting system receives regular ongoing maintenance performs successfully over many years.

A new approach for improving the energy efficiency and afforadability of solar energy in building is gaining wide attention of the researchers in this field; namely the hybrid solar lighting and full spectrum systems. This concept views solar energy from a dynamic, systems-level perspective, integrates multiple inter-dependent technologies, and makes better use of the entire solar energy spectrum. On a real time basis by using different portions of the solar spectrum simultaneously for multiple and use applications in buildings, the system offers unique advantages over the traditional approaches of harnessing the sun's light and energy. According to Muhs, Head, Department of US Energy's Oak Ridge National Laboratory (2000), "Unlike conventional solar energy approaches that convert sunlight into electricity and pay the price of photovoltaic inefficiency, hybrid lighting uses sunlight directly into electricity. Roof-mounted collectors concentrate sunlight into optional fibres that carry the light inside buildings to hybrid light fixtures that also contain electric lamps." The hybrid solar light systems also overcomes a number of limitations of passive daylighting systems of today, such as spatial and temporal variability, glare, excess illumination, cost and energy efficiency. The new approach suggests that the most appropriate use of the visible portion of direct, non-diffuse sunlight from a energy saving perspective is to displace electric light rather than generate electricity.

6. Lighting maintenance

All lighting systems experience deterioration of performance during operation. Aged fluorescent tubes, after three or four years of use, may still function but may produce only 60 per cent or less of the light they produced when new, while still consuming the same amount of energy and generating the same amount of unwanted heat. "As many as 300 to 400 million kilowatt-hour of electricity is being wasted every day or light that is absorbed by dust and dirt, by old bulbs and tubes that have outlived their usefulness, and on extra lighting capacity that a new study says is no longer needed" says US National lighting Bureau chairman, Cary S.Mendelsohn. Most of the times lighting systesms are maintained in a reactive rather than proactive manner. Lamps are replaced as they fail, defective components such as failed ballasts and broken lamp holders are only replaced when they cause fixture to malfunction, and fixtures are rarely cleared, although dirt and dust buildup is absorbing useful light rather than distributing it. Replacing fluorescent tubes and other lighting sources on a planned, routine basis can contribute so much to better lighting and energy savings that the amount of money saved can dwarf whatever savings are derived from replacing tubes and bulbs only after they burn out. Although they may still function after three or four years of use, these aged fluorescent may produce only 60 per cent or less of the light they produced when new. Worse, their low light output could impact lighting quality to the extent that productivity and safety could be comprised.

Considering the waste in labour and energy costs involved, its generally advisible to consider a planned lighting maintenance programme during the planning of the lighting system. Planned lighting maintance is the practice of organising labour and resources to ensure consistent recommended light levels and prevention of wasteful energy expenditure. It constutes three actions to be taken on periodic basis : group relamping, fixture cleaning, and inspection and trouble shooting. Planned maintance strategies can: (i) reduce nominal labour costs related to fixture relamping and cleaning by up to 70 per cent, (ii) reduce cost by concentrating lamp purchases into fewer, high-volume buys, (iii) produce higher light levels over the life of the lighting system, (iv) generate lighting upgrade opportunities such as reduced-output energy-saving lamps that take advantage of higher light levels to reduce energy costs and (V) ensure proper inspection and upkeep of the lighting system, such as ensuring batteries are charged for emergency lighting in compliance with regulations.

Conclusion

The past decade has provided the widest variety and most interesting arsenal of low wattage, compact, colour-improved, energy saving light sources and highly sophisticated energy management lighting control systems. Architects and lighting designers have contributed tremendously into the design development of energy-sensitive lighting systems with respect to both electric and day lighting. The paper supports and encourages the design community to pursue and promote eco-friendly lighting design services to its residential, commercial and industrial customers. Energy efficiency needs to be installed at a basic level by creating proper support system so that energy-efficient lighting could become a common practice and hence, any policy formulated to deal with energy conservation will have to be highly innovative and make indigenous investment devices strategies for look for energy planning must ensure the following considerations so that every energy component within technological grasp can be employed in every lighting project.

1. Public awareness : Effects need to be directed towards public information campaigns that would create awareness and educate the general consumers about economic and environmental benefits of energy - efficient lighting.

2. Educating lighting professionals : Lighting designers and consultants need to be educated about the responsibility they hold towards contributing to a sustainable environment and how they could fulfill this responsibility through the use of energy sensitive lighting technology and designs.

3. Quality assurance : Standards need to be established for quality specifications of various lighting products to guarantee the reliability of their performance to the consumers.

4. Creating product identity : There is a need to initiate a quality labelling programme to enable consumers to recognize high-quality products, and to provide the energy-efficient lighting equipment an identity of environment - friendly products.

5. Removing financial barriers : Financing or leasing programmes need to be developed to help consumers to over come the initial high cost of purchasing energy - efficient technology instead of less expensive conventional lighting products, through provision of fiscal benefits, subsidies and soft loans. Investment advisory firms and financial intermediaries can work out on various innovative financing tools that allow the capital costs of lighting efficiency improvements to be paid for out of energy-savings.

6. Creating market support system : Energy efficiency needs to be installed at a basic level by creating proper support system so that energy- efficient lighting could become a common practice. This could be done in terms of ; (i) developing efficient lighting product manufacturing and distribution infrastructure, (ii) creating co-operative market building activities, such as promotional price discounts and joint marketing-efforts, (iii) co-ordinating bulk purchases of energy-efficient lighting as a way to reduce unit cost and create new market and (iv) identifying regulatory barriers that make it difficult for manufactures of energy-efficient lighting equipment to compete e.g. high sales taxes or import tariffs and developing strategies for gradually removing them.

REFERENCES

Bhattacharya, S. and Mitra, A.P. (Eds.) (1998), Greenhouse Gas Emissions in India for the Base year 1990 : Global Change Scientific Report NO.11, May 1998, New Delhi : National Physical Laboratory.

Craig, D. and Randy, S. 2000 "Introduction to lighting maintance" *www. lightiningdesignlab.com/articles/maintance*

Energy Information Administration (2001), "India Environmental Issues,"*www.eia.doe.gov.*

Gupta, V. (1992), "Energy conservation in office buildings" Architecture + Design, May-June 1992, pp. 57-59.

Jaju, N. and George, R. (2001), "Energy efficient lighting technology : an option for controlling environmental pollution", Proceding of 8th National Conference of IWSA-2001, Pune.

Lediner N. (1991), "Heating, cooling, Lighting Design Methods for Architects, New York : John Wiley and Sons, pp. 318-335.

Leslie, R.P. (1991), "Listening to lightings music", Ld+A, March 1991, p.11.

Leslie, R.P. (1994), "What makes daylight successful?" CADDET Energy Efficiency Newsletter No.4, pp. 4-6.

Lesile, R.P. and Conway, K.M. (1996), The Lighting Pattern Book for Homes, New York : McGraw Hill Company Inc., pp. 188-202.

Mendelsohn, C.S. (2000) "Emphasize maintance to conserve electricity", *www.lighting.com.*

Muhs, J. (2000), "Design and analysis of hybrid solar lighting and full-spectrum solar energy systems", Proceedings of American Solar Energy Society's Solar 2000 Conference, Madison, Wisconsin, June 16-21,

Plas, R.V.D. (1998), "Rural PV lighting : opportunity lost?" IAEEL News letter. 7, (21) pp.6-9.

Vera, T. (1992), "Energy awareness", LD+A, February, 1992, p. 21.

"Residential PV applications" *www.worldbank. org/fpd/energy/subsenergy/solar/residential.htm.*

6

Remedies in Our Hand for Controlling Air Pollution Because of Urban Traffic

Yogesh T. Jasrai

Problem of pollution as a consequence of increased industrialization is by now a well known phenomenon. In fact this is more prominent specially in cities because of the population growth which is due to both immigration from rural areas and to the natural increase in urban population itself. However, there is another factor-the automobiles causing an air pollution, more in cities. The number of vehicles on the road has increased to an enormous number posing a threat to human survival not due to accidents but more because of the polluted air. This because of excessive dependence on automobiles, ill-regulated traffic and roads. In lieu of polluted water and contaminated food one can use bottled water or aerated drinks and packaged food respectively. However, for polluted air there is no alternative. Probably, days are not too far when we will get bottled fresh air in the market. In facts, Oxygen parlours have already come-up in several cities to help stressed individuals. The following points need to be taken into consideration for checking air pollution from automobiles in cities.

Cross roads

Construction of multistorey buildings to be avoided right at the cross roads. Rather, part of the cross road corners must be kept open without any construction, so that plants can be grown in different tiers of herbs, shrubs and trees. The central area of cross roads in form of circle should be kept to the maximum so as to give enough space for the traffic exhaust to get dissipated. At the cross roads, between to and fro lanes, *Polyalthia* pendula can be planted which grow straight without affecting the passage of vehicles. Alternately, *Bogainvillea* can also be planted. Between the lanes one can also arrange large potted plants which can be replaced at regular intervals.

More preference should be given for construction of single point shopping complex. This will ensure one point shopping of almost all essential commodities. However, an efficient and enough/ open parking place need to be provided. Alternately, shopping arenas need to be planned right at the residential localities.

Use of Vehicles

Engine of vehicles need to be upgraded so that they can work on lead-less petrol or more efficient, less smoke fuel. The exhaust point need to be raised on top of the vehicles or provided with filters. New forms of transport need to be designed that are fuel/energy efficient, non-polluting and tailored to our needs.

Conversely, there need to be more efficient, well planned and economical public transport system so as to transport more passengers. This will discourage people using their own 2/4 wheeler and in turn will reduce the traffic load on the roads. Sometime, one can also look for transport on sharing basis. For short distance movements people must use bicycles. This well help not only in reducing consumption of fuel but also a good exercise for the individuals. Road side parking should be strictly prohibited and parking areas need to be planned at regular points so that people can move on foot for shopping in our traditional long stretched, narrow lane markets.

For all these actions, a strict legislation must be enforced so as to check pollution from auto exhausts, parking etc. by the lawful officials.

Article No. 6

Pl. 1.Polyalthia longifolia
Benth. & HK.f.

Pl. 2.Bougainvillea spectabilis.

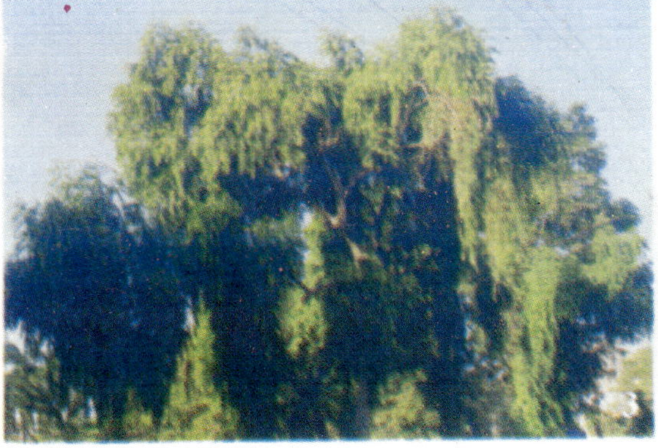

Pl. 3.Putranjiva roxburghii Wall.

Pl. 4.Millingtonia
hortensis L.

Road Side Planning

Fast growing trees like *Peltophorum/Cassia/*Neem/*Cassia fistula* etc. can be planted on all road sides. The plants specially with long boles like *Eucalyptus/Polyalthia* pendula etc. can be planted if the space available is less on the road sides and between the lanes.

Trees like *Spathodea, Millingtonia, Dalbargia, Ficus, Pongamia,Putranjiva, Tamarindus,Alstonia, Cassia fistula* etc. can be planted as avenue trees to impart a scenic beauty to the spots.

After planting trees they need to be protected with tree-guards. Such guards can further be covered by gunny-bags or old banners so as to protect the planted saplings from animals specially goat and this in turn makes the plant to grow faster.

In case of road-side buildings having their verandas on roads one can put climbers which will not only act as filter for dust but also picks up air pollutants.

With recent spurt in urbanization and industrilization the increase in vehicular pollution has become alarming. In fact, long-back legislation has been enacted as the Air (Prevention and Control of Pollution) Act, 1981. However, law is not the only answer to abate pollution challenge. It is merely a tool for the people.. Therefore, our determination and real participation in implementing the suggested actions and generating the awareness among the masses will help in protecting our environment.

REFERENCES

Chakraverty R. K. and Jain S. K. (1984) Beautiful Trees and Shrubs of Calcutta, BSI, Howrah.

Santapau H. (1987) common Trees, National Book Trust, New Delhi.

7

Eco-friendly Approach To Control Fungal Biodeteriogens

Arun Arya, N.R. Shah, Chitra Arya and Chinmoyee Dash

Biodeterioration

Fungi cause diseases in plants, animals and human beings. These can cause deterioration of Museum materials. Fungal growth can ultimately result into—

a) Stains, foxing and discolouration on paper and cloth materials.

b) Disfigurement and powdering of the materials.

c) Reduction of the strength of the wood or leather thus reducing their life.

Biodeterioration and its control are one of the very important aspects of conservation of cultural property. To avoid the irreparable damage by microbes use of preventive measures and control strategies are suggested by numerous workers from time to time. Modern scientific developments are in no way less than miracles but simultaneously they have also augmented the element of risk to human life. Much reliance on the modern chemical advancement has to some extent crippled the progress of our indigenous traditio-nal ways of protecting our cultural property. The use of synthetic pesticides has brought with them the problems of environmental pollution and other undesirable sides effects, harming the normal life cycle of human beings and animals as well. The cost of the synthetic pesticides is also very high. Increasing sensitivity in animal world towards the ill effects of these chemicals is sufficient to make us extra cautious while using them. The increasing resistance among the target pests also demands other alternatives. Use of botanical pesticide is one of such probable alternatives. These biodegradable, non-pollutive chemicals are screened and their anti-microbial action is reported.

In the present paper use of bitter gourd (*Momordica charantia* L.) as an antifungal agent is reported. The antifungal property of fruit pulp, epicarp (fruit peeling) and seeds of Karela was determined by poisoned food technique. The fruit peeling gave the promising results. Of the four fungal biodeteriogens tried *Myrothecium roridum* could not grow at 25% concentration.

Introduction

The control of biodeterioration of cultural property is a very complex affair. Besides preventive measures, chemical,biological and radiological control methods are available. Use of IPM is suggested, because effect of chemicals on museum objects and environment is not fully understood. Indiscriminate use of chemicals may lead to development of resistance in biodeteriogens.

The commonly used synthetic fungicide have been found to display sides effects in form of carcinogenicity, teratogenicity and pollutive effects. Use of less harmful and true eco-friendly products of plant origin are replacing the routine fungicides (Fawcett and Spencer 1969, Khanna and Chandra 1972, Dixit *et al.* 1983, Arya and Mathew 1990, Arya *et al.* 1995). Efforts are on to find out substitutes for chlorine containing, pentachlorophenol, ethylene dioxide, Gammexane and Dieldrin like pesticides. Use of synthetic pesticide is increasing day by day to meet the challanges of agriculture sector. Modern scientific developments are in no way less than concern with the health of common man.

The Botanical pesticides like pyrethrum, rotenone, ryania and nicotine were in vogue before the advent of synthetic pesiticides, but thereafter, these botanicals were relegated to insignificant position in pest control. Pyrethrum is extracted from flowers of *Chrysenthemum cinerieolium* and rotenone is derived from rhizomes of *Derris* and *Lonchorpus*. It has been used as fish poison (Munshi, 1995). Neem is the most promising source of biopesticide. Neem owes its toxic attributes to a large number of bitter compounds called Meliacins like azadirachtin, nimbin, salannin, meliantriol etc. Neem seed kernels are richest source of meliacins and contain 0.2-0.3% azadirachtin and 30-40% oil. Though neem leaves and seed contain azadirachtin, bark also contains this yet in smaller quantities. George (1999) reported Swallow root (*Decalepis hamiltonii*) of family Asclepiadaceae causing protection of food grains against insect infestation. Rice borer (*Sitophilus oryzae*) and Rust red flour beetle (*Tribolium*) were controlled by the application of Swallowrot. Inhibition of fungal growth was observed on garlic extract (Tansy and Appleton 1975). Electron microscopic studies revealed thickening in cell wall in *Rhizoctonia solani,* whereas, *Colletorichum lindemuthianum* revealed a singular accumulation of osmiophill bodies immediately under the cell membrane when subjected to suspension of micronized garlic powder in distilled water (Bianchi *et al.* 1997).

The Smithsonian museum consits of 11 exhibition buildings in Washington D.C. and New York city. Two of the most popular exhibition buildings with the public are National Museum of Natural History and the newest National Air and Space museum. The presence of Whale skeleton is also there as in Baroda Museum (Roy 1982). The Musee de la civilzation, a public museum was built in 1988. It is located in the capital city of Quebec province in Canada. The museum is based on central theme of the Person and the Human Experience. Disseminating information, explaining, reaching out to a large number of people and broadening their sphere of knowledge, were among the priorities set by this museum of Canada (Hamel 1999). It holds exhibition on different themes. Origin of Man was one such exhibition, where, how man discovered to cultivate cereals? and how to know the time etc.? were shown in Sept-Oct.2003.

Many of the articles are made of wood or metals in a museum on paper, leather and cloth in a library. Museum materials are attacked by a variety of fungi. The museum objects are organic in nature, some times made of objects like palm leaf, as in manuscripts the objects may be of leather as well as in various ethnological objects or in taxidermy objects they are of different nature. All these offer opportunity for growth of a great variety of fungal flora. During routine survey isolated bio-pollutants included species of *Aspergillus, Pencillium, Mucor, Rhizopus, Alternaria, Helminthosporium, Drechslera, Cladosporium, Monilia* etc. The present study was undertaken

Table : Effect of seed, fruit peeling and pulp of *Momordica charantia* on four fungal biodeteriogens.

SI. No.	*Treatments*	*Conc. %*	*Myrotheci um*	*Chaetomi um*	*Phoma*	*Eurotium*
			Dia. (mm.)*	Dia. (mm.) *	Dia. (mm.)	Dia. (mm.)
1.	Seed	0	80	80	65	55
2.	"	5	75	75	35	45
3.	"	10	55	32	50	27
4.	"	25	25	25	00	00
5.	Fruit plup	0	70	75	60	50
6.	"	5	75	70	55	30
7.	"	10	50	50	35	25
8.	"	25	20	35	20	00
9.	Fruit peel-ing	0	70	75	65	50
10.	"	5	55	70	55	30
11.	"	10	25	30	25	25
12.	"	25	00	00	10	20

* Readings representing average of five replicates, Dia. = Diametre

to assess the anti-fungal potential of different parts of bitter gourd.

Materials and Methods

The anti-fungal property of bitter gourd was tested using Poisoned food technique (Nene and Thapliyal 1979). The Karela fruits were procured from local market. It was separated in to three parts:

1. seeds
2. fruit pulp
3. peelings of fruit (the uneven green part).

Hundred gram of each part was crushed and mixed with 100 ml distilled water and 100 ml extract was obtained in each case. Desired concentration of bitter gourd extract was prepared and mixed with PDA medium to make final volume 100 ml and it was autoclaved. Then it was poured in 100mm petriplates and test fungi were inoculated in the center.

Effect of four fungal pathogens namely *Myrothecium roridum* Tode ex Fr., *Chaetomium ganglegarum* L. Ames, *Phoma multirostrata* Mathur and *Eurotium chevalieri* Mangin was observed after inoculating them for 8 days at 25 ± 2^0C. Radial colony diameter at two different places was taken. Results thus obtained are recorded in Table 1. Earlier the *Chaetomium gangleg-erum* was isolated from painting in Boroda Museum (Arya *et al.* 1988), *Myrothecium roridum* was obtained from Herbarium sheet preserved in Botany department (Arya and Arya communicated). *M. roridum* is a biopollutant and a fruit rot pathogen. It has been reported causing soft rot of guava (Rai *et al.* 1982).

Results and Discussion

This common fruit vegetable Karela (Bitter gourd) belongs to the family Cucurbitaceae. The fruits are ribbed, fusiform containing many compressed brown seeds. The bitter principles of the fruit are alkaloid momordicine present in many compressed brown seeds. The bitter principles of the fruit are alkoloid momordicine (0.038%) and some saponines (Sabnis and Daniel 1990). The seeds and fruit wall of *M. charantia* contain Elaterin a (cucurbitacin) and alkaloids that cause sever vomiting and diarrhoea. A protein from bitter melon has been shown in laboratory to Kill HIV infected cells causing cellular toxicity.

Fruit peelings were effective in two cases. Seeds of bitter gourd were effective in two cases. *Phoma* and *Eurotium* could not grow at 25% conc. of seed extract. It is noteworthy that we discard these parts due to bitter taste, which can be collected and used to prepare an antifungal powder. Of the four fungal biodeteriogens tried *M. roridum* and *C. ganglegarum* could not grew at 25% concentration of fruit peelings.

Acknowledgements

Thanks are due to Prof. G.P. Senan, Head, Department of Botany for provinding laboratory facilities and to Prof. A.K. Sarbhoy, IARI,New Delhi for providing identification of fungal cultures.

REFERENCES

Arya, A., Chauhan, R. and Arya, C. 1995, Effect of allicin and extracts of garlic and *Bignonia* on two fungi. *Indian J. Mycol* and *Pl. Pathol.* 25(3) : 316-318.

Bianchi, A., Zambonelli, A.D., Aulerio, A.Z. and Bellesia, F., 1997, Ultrastrucural studies of the effects of *Allium sativum. Plant Disease* 81 (11) : 1241-1246.

Chander, S. and Munshi, A.D. 1995, Botonical Pesticides. *Employment news* 20(39) : 1-2

Dixit, S.N., Dubey, N.K. and Tripathi, N.N., 1983, Fungitoxic oils vis a vis disease control,In *Recent advances* in *Plant Path*. Eds. Husain, A., Singh, K., Singh, B.P. and Agnihotri, V.P. Print House India Lucknow pp. 521.

Fawcett, C.H. and Spencer, D.M., 1970, *Ann Rev. Phytopath.* 8:403-418

George, J., Ravishankar, G.A., Pereira, J. and Divakar, S., 1999, Bioinsecticide from swallow root (*Decalepis hamiltonii* Wight & Arn) protects food grains against insect infestation *Curr. Sci.* 77(4) 501-502.

Hamel, P., 1999, *This is a Museum.* Pub by Musee De La Civilization, Quebec City 24 pp.

Khanna, K.K. and Chandra, S., 1972, Antifungal activity in some plant extracts. *Proc. Nat. Acad. Sci. India* 42(B)300-302.

Nene, Y.L. and Thapliyal, P.N., 1979 *Fungicides in plant disease control.* Oxf. And IBH Publ. Co. New Delhi, 507pp.

Rai, R.N. Lal, B. and Arya, A., 1982, Some New Fruit rot diseases. *Indian J. Mycol. Pl. Pathol* 12: 264-266

Roy, S., 1982, The many sided Smithsonian. *Span* 23(4) : 22-27

Sabnis, S.D. and Daniel, M., 1990, *A Phytochemical approach to Economic Botany.* Kalyani pub. Ludhiana. pp

Tansey, M.R. and Appleton, J.A., 1975, Inhibition of fungal growth by garlic extract.*Mycologia* 67 : 409-413.

Zhang, Q.C., 1992, Preliminary report on the use of *Momordica charantia* extract by HIV patient. *J. Naturopth Med.* 3: 65-69.

8

Urban Air Pollution, Health And Role Of Developmental Communication

Anjali Pahad and Avani Maniar

Air is found everywhere and it is the most important component of the enviroment. Air may get polluted by natural causes such as volcanic activity, which releases ash, dust, sulphur compounds etc. or forest and grass fires caused by lightning, and/or through man-made causes such as industrial activities, transportation etc.

Modern environemental threats like acid rain, global warming, ozone depletion and smog formation, etc. are the results of air pollution. Not only the human beings, but the aniamls and plants are also adversely affected by air pollution. Air pollution levels in several major cities in the West are going down, while in India, they are going up. The sulphur dioxide and particulate matter in several Inidian cities has already exceeded permissible limits set by the World Health Organization. Delhi is the tenth most polluted city in the world. According to a study by Central Road Research Institute in 1998, vehicles generated 64 percent of the total pollution laod in Delhi. The rest was by industries and power plants. The sources and effects of air pollution are varied and complex. Two main sources of man-made air pollution are vehicular emissions and industrial processes.

a) Vehicles

There has been a tremendous increase in the number of motorized vehicles in the past few decades. In urban India, each adult member of a family has a vehicle. Before children attain the age of 18 years, they start driving a two wheeler. All these vehicles run on petrol or diesel, which are fossil fuels. The burning of fossil fuels, and their incomplete combustion in engines, leads to the release of a number of polluting gases into the atmosphere. Some of these such as carbon monoxide, carbon dioxide, nitrogen oxides, oxides of sulphur, hydrocarbons, lead, etc. have serious ill effects on human health, on vegetation, materials, etc. In most towns and cities, when vehicular traffic is heavy in the evenings, atmosphere appears hazy due to photochemical smog, which affects eyes and the respiratory system.

b) Industries

Mushrooming industries, right in the midst of the residential areas, are the main causes of air pollution. Industries discharge pollutants which not only contain smoke and soot, but other particualte as well as gaseous pollutants. They affect human beings, flora and fauna, soil, water and man-made structures. The amount of toxic substances released within a factory, is very harmful for the people who work or live near such industrial plants.

Health effects of Air Pollution

A primary reason for wanting clean air is that polluted air can damage human health. Ozone formed in photochemical smog has been linked to a number of health problems. Volunteers who were exposed to high levels of ozone, experienced chest pains and persistent coughing. Their lung cpapacity also declined, so they could not breathe well. Ozone also appears to aggravate chronic respiratory problems such as asthma, bronchitis, and emphysema, lung conditions that cause difficulty in breathing. Studies have also found that some 20% of healthy individuals are usally sensitive to ozone, for no apparent reason.

When inhaled, carbon monoxide impairs the blood's ability to deliver oxygen to bodily tissues. At high concentrations, it can be fatal. Slightly higher carbon monoxide level can trigger heart attacks. Sulphur dioxide can cause serious health problems, particularly in combination with particulates. Alone, it can irritate the lungs and aggravate respiratory diseases such as bronchitis. It can also cause damage when it combines with water vapour to form sulfuric acid droplets. More serious damage appears when solid particles combine with sulphur dioxide in air to form sulphates which damage lung tissue if inhaled.

Another air pollutant that poses a serious health hazard is lead, which can accumulate in the body over time and cause serious damage to kidneys, immune system, blood forming organs, and nervous sytem. Fossil fuel combustion produces many pollutants including nitrogen oxides, sulfur oxides, hydrocarbons, mercury and particulates. These pollutants can cause serious health problems including asthma, irritation of the lungs, bronchitis, pneumonia, decreased resistance to respiratory injections, and even early death.

Human health will be affected if carbon dioxide levels continue to increase. The planet will become warmer in the next century, which may result in more heat-related illness, more severe weather events, floods and droughts, and an increase in cases of vector-borne and water-borne diseases.

Some air pollutants are toxic like benzene, organic compounds such as dioxin and metals. These pollutants are known or suspected to cause cancer or other serious health effects, such as repreductive effects or birth defects, or adverse environmental effects. Environment education is crucial for all the citizens, to bring environment and development concerns to peoples' notice, to enable them to understand the linkages, between the two, to encourage them to take appropriate action, and to equip them with the skills necessary for taking the required action.

In India, environmental education is imparted through school and college curriculum, government organizations, non government organizations, voluntary organizations and mass media. At present, the need of the hour is not only to impart environment education but motivate people to take positive actions towards betterment of environment. Here, the role of development communicator is important.

Role of Development Communicator

Development communicator is a link between the source-experts, scientists and bureaucrats and the receivers at the grass root level. Therefore, he has to play an important role in facilitating communication process for development. He is like a catalytic agent in the development process. He works in a human laboratory, where different perspectives are required for working with people. He has to develop people centred vision of development and act as development facilitator bringing people together in order to do any development programme. He has to create an environment for transactional communication and constructive interaction. Thus, he has to stimulate people at grass root level to work and take initiative for their own development. To save ourselves from such environmental hazards, we will have to work together on the issue. Hence, community participation has a lot of relevance here.

The term community participation is being increasingly used for social welfare and health programmes. However, attempts have been made to understand community participations as conscious process, which should be built around specific groups of people rather than and ideal state to be achieved directly by the imple-mentation of programmes. Community participation can be in

* Decision making to improve community health.
* Community demand for improved and relevant health services, and
* Social control over health services.

Positive broad strategies are mentioned here, which will help in community participation

1. Community Mobilization :

The community should be mobilized around various programmes such as issues of urban pollution's education etc. These should be on sporadic basis and should sustain over a period of time. This will let people gain access to the issues and their solutions and subsequently can put pressure on the goverment to provide improved programmes.

2. Empowerment:

This mass ability of members of the community to move from 'I can't to 'we can'. Empowerment enables communities to work collectively for common interests. There are many evidences of intencive educational efforts for empowerment in many NGO projects.

3. Structural Strategies :

Structural strategies are used to promote community participation like Mahila Mandals, youth groups, eco clubs. These prove to be an effective forum for promoting participation in curbing the pollution related problems in cities.

4. Financing :

It is believed that if people pay, even partially for such issues, they have more faith and interest in the programmes and a greater desire to ensure the relevance and effectiveness of services provided.

5. Training :

Training is adopted as a multi-pronged strategy to promote community participation. People are identified from community and are trained to articulate the health needs and interests of the member of the community and as facilitator to enhance access to health care.

Educational Interventions

Evidence suggests that fostering community participation

through an educational intervention which focuses on enhancing health awareness of the members of the community has a longer sustaining potential. Non-formal education efforts by non government organizations and educational institutions like, the Department of Home Science Extension and Communication, Faculty of Home Science, M.S. University, Baroda, are a starting point, for implementing such programmes, as we spend considerable time in understanding people's problems, their experiences, their needs, attitudes and perceptions.

Skill Building

Deliberate efforts should be made to build skills of the members of the community in order to strengthen their role in the health programmes. Building skills to analyze the situation, cropping up is a necssary precondition for the community to get involved in the subsequent stages of programme development. Similarly building skills in decision making is a precondition for its active participation in programmes. Skill building also includes the development of technical skills that are necessary for providing health services.

Policy Implications

Some of the key implications for promoting and sustaining health related programmes in terms of a policy making framework are :

1. A multiplicity of approaches should be encouraged.
2. Deliberate interventions are needed. Resources are necessarily required to implement these interventions like finance, place, infrastructure, experts, etc.
3. Financing-builds accountability of the programme to the community.
4. Ensure flexibility in the planning and implementation of programmes so that they are relevant to local context.
5. Organizational culture—which is characterized by purposiveness, flexibility, sensitivity and a learning orientation can sustain community involvement. Many

non goverment organizations have tried to build in such organizational culture and have proved successful too. But goverment should also adopt such strategies.

* The gigantic size of government infrastructure.
* Over reliance on target achievement.
* Uniformity of practices.
* Excessive adherence to rules and norms.

could make it difficult to promote and sustain authentic peoples' involvement in government programmes.

REFERENCES

1. Frandes, Walter (ed.) People's participation in Development, Indian Social Intitute, New Delhi. 1980.
2. Ghai, Dharam. Participatory Development, United Nations Research Institute for Social Development, Geneva, 1988.
3. Rehman, Anisur (ed.) Grassroot participation and Self Reliance, Oxford, India Book House and Society fo Participatory Research in Asia, New Delhi, 1984.
4. Viswanath, L.S. People's Organization for Rural Development, Mainstream, New Delhi. 27th July, 1992.

9

An Overview of Fine Particulate Pollution

Indranil Mukherjee, Biswajit Thakur, Anupam Dev Sarkar and Shibnath Chakrabarty

It is a well-established fact that mortality and morbidity has a direct correlation with high particulate concentration in the ambient air. Particulate pollution is the major contributor behind the sufferings of city dwellers all over the world from various cardio-pulmonary diseases. Since, finer fractions of Respirable Particulate Matter (RPM) is more likely to invade deeper into the respiratory tracts and accumulate there, it is presently being considered as the most dangerous of the particulate pollutant species. This paper deals with various aspects of fine particulate [$PM_{2.5}$]. pollution. It unfolds the probable sources and origins of fine particulates [$PM_{2.5}$], their major types and pollution problems associated with them. Both the health effects and visibility impairment have been discussed with some typical examples. The steps taken internationally to combat this pollution problem have also been discussed.

1.0 Introduction

Particulate is a very important pollutant with respect to its health effect. The severity of the effect depends upon the degree of advancement of particulate matter within the respiratory tract (refer to figure-1) and its associated effects. From the figure-1, it is evident that upto a certain size, lesser the aerodynamic diameter more is the percentage rentention within the body. The residence time for these particulates is also very high, i.e., once engulfed by the body system, the particulates have the tendency to remain within the body system for a long period of time. Thus it can be concluded that size is one of the criteria to assess the probable health effects. There in lies the importance of the fine particulates with respect to the health point of view. Thus proper monitoring of fine particulate matter is necessary, Subsequently, after the establishment of a proper data inventory, decision is needed to be taken regarding the inclusion of $PM_{2.5}$ into the National Ambient Air Quality Standards (NAAQS). The Standards established must be stringent enough,and any value exceeding these prescribed values must be taken as a direct indication of a highly polluted unhealthy environment to survive.

2.0 Source of Fine Particulates

To get proper idea regarding the major contributors to fine particulates, the sources of them are needed to be identified. There are three major origins of fine particulates and are discussed one by one as follows :

Primary solid particulate matter that is emitted directly into the solid phase is a significant category fine particulates. It results largely from combustion of fossil fuels in automobiles and industrial processes, wood combustion, land clearing and wild fires. It also incorporates fugitive emissions from paved and unpaved roads, dust from ore processing and refining, and to a lesser extent, crustal material from construction activties, agricultural tilling, wind erosion etc.

The second category comprises of primary condensable particulate that can be emitted at high temperatures in the gaseous phase condensing into the solid phase upon dilution and cooling in the plume. They are largely made up of semi-volatile organic compounds. This condensable component represents a significant fraction of the fine particulates. Researches are going on to charecterize the condensable fractions more completely and with greater accuracy.

Secondary particulate that is formed through atmospheric reactions of gaseous Sulfur Dioxide (SO_2) and Oxides of Nitrogen (NOx) precursor emissions forms the third category of fine particulates. Secondary $PM_{2.5}$ forms through heterogeneous (gas to particle) chemical reactions that convert some gaseous pollutants into very small particles. The observed secondary $PM_{2.5}$ is dominated by Sulfate and Nitrate species in most locations, however, there can also be significant contributions from Secondary Organic Aerosol (SOA) in some locations.

Sulfate aerosol chemistry can involve either gas-phase or liquid-phase oxidation processes. Gas phase conversion involves the oxidation of SO_2 by hydroxyl radicals, which are formed due to the photodecomposition of ozone. the reaction results in sulfuric acid aerosol as an airborne particle with a typical aerodynamic diameter of less than 0.3 microns (and thus within the $PM_{2.5}$ range). The sulfuric acid particles are then neutralized by ammonia and molecular oxygen to form ammonium bi sulphate and ammonium sulfate. Liquid phase reactions involve SO_2 and oxidants like H_2O_2, O_3 nascent oxygen (O^x), along with catalysts, such as manganese and iron, that are dissolved in cloud or fog droplets to form sulfuric acid aerosols with diameters in the range of 0.5 to 1.0 microns.

There are different ways by which the nitrates can be formed. The most important pathway is the gas-phase reaction of NO_2 with hydroxyl radicals to produce nitiric acid, which is then neutralized by the gaseous ammonia. When the levels of ammonia and nitric acid are sufficiently high, ammonium nitrate can be formed within the $PM_{2.5}$ size range (Frandes, 1980).

3.0 Health Effects of Fine Particulates

The fine particulates account for a substantial impact on human health and the quality of human environment. The human respiratory system acts as a highly effective filter for coarse particles, removing a large percentage of those inhaled particles of an aerodynamic diameter greater than 2.5 microns. On the contrary the fine particulates of less than equals to 2.5 microns in aerodynamic diameter are capable of penetrating deep into the lungs and accumulating there where their physical presence can increase airway resistance and susceptibility to infection, and reduce lung function. In case of severe exposure to fine particulates diseases like fibrosis and sillicosis can occur. Even if these particulates are chemically inert, they can act as irritants and can impair lung function severely. In recent toxicological and epidemiological studies, observable health effects have been found to be associated with exposure to respirable sized particles. In addition the fine particulates tend to worsen the effects of gaseous pollutant materials when present together.

The size of the particulate mattter is the most important consideration that determines their penetration into the human respiratory system. There are three basic mechanisms of aerosol deposition namely inertial impaction, sedimentation and diffusion of which the later two are responsible for the deposition of fine particualtes. The sedimentation mechanism is most prevalent in the trachea and in the bronchial region where inhaled particles in diameter range of 1-5 microns are most effectively deposited. Diffusive deposition is most common in the alveolar region and is responsible for the deposition of particles smaller than 0.5 microns in diameter. Particles deposited in the alveoli may persist there for as long as a year. In the alveolar region a significant fraction of the particles may enter the interstices. Particles can be transported into the lymphatic system or circulatory system to other organs of the body. Materials may reach and accumulate in any target organ or may be excreted via natural pathways. Very small particles less than .01 microns do not accumulate on lung surface; instead they are absorbed by body fluids.

The specificiy to the cardiovascular and respiratory mortality reflects the role of particulate matter especially $PM_{2.5}$ and the biological systems with which it is more closely associated. The significant difference between the effect on the lower respiratory system and the upper respiratory system appears to reflect the highter toxicity of $PM_{2.5}$ that travels deeper into the respiratory tract.

Although there are no experimentally established mechanisms for a $PM_{2.5}$ effect, one possible mechanism can be inferred from the mode of action of man made mineral fibers (MMMF). MMMF are fibrous inorganic materials, mainly derived from rock, clay, or glass filament. Size ranges from 0.1 to 100 microns. In response to the foreign particles, the immunity systems engulfs the $PM_{2.5}$ with macrophages in the lung. Chemically activated alveolar macrophages, a condition that would exist after long- term exposure to $PM_{2.5}$, activate so called the mediators, which increase the inflammatory response. These mediators, in conjunction with epithelial cells, release polypetide growth factors, which stimulate the proliferation of mesenchymal cells. Mesenchymal cells are precursor cells that produce cell lines involved in the immune defense response. The unnaturally high number of mesenchymal cells produce cytokinens, which ultimately increase the local inflammatory response. The immune response reaches such a point that it injures the alveolar capillay membrane. This results in an effective decrease in the number of working alveoli, which are responsible for O_2/CO_2 gas exchange. Thus lung capacity and efficiency is decreased. The lung is literally scarred internally by the magnitude of immune response to conditions of high concen-tration of foreign particles.

Another efffect as referred to by the immunologists is the non-sense response. The highly activated macrophages may be inhibited in their capacity for specific response to other foreign bodies. An illustrative example is that, those suffering from sillicosis appear to have an increased proclivity for the development of tuberculosis. The epidemiologists expect that a series of steps may be necessary following deposition of fine particulates in the lungs before most physiological and clinical effects can be observed.

4.0 Other Adverse Effects of Fine Particulates

In addition to the direct effects of this fine particulate matter on human health, it may alter the human environment in a variety of ways. Many of these effects will degrade human health indirectly or affect human welfare.

Fine particulate matter, particularly if it contains sulphate or nitrate, is the principal conveyor of acid in the atmosphere. Fine particulates play an important role, not only in the air pollution and degradation of materials, but also in long-term impacts on the acidity of fresh water bodies and soils. One area, which will receive increasing attention, will be the impact on the geochemical balance of acidity and sulphur and its relation to the long-term productivity of natural and agricultural soils.

The fine particulate matters ($PM_{2.5}$) contribute largely to the impairment of visibility in the atmosphere. They can cause significant effects on the light transmission characteristics of the atmosphere. These fine particulates cause changes in the optical properties of the atmosphere and there by causing absorption and scattering of light rays in the atomsphere.

Eventually, the presence of these fine particultes in the atmosphere alters the fundamental chemical and physical properties of the atmosphere in ways that are very difficult to comprehend. Heat transfer rates, the formation of precipitation, the static electrical properties of the atmosphere and other phenomena are all significantly changed by these fine particulates.(Y.N. report)

5.0 Present Scenario of Fine Particulate Pollution :

In the following paragraphs the grave scenario of fine particulate pollution in India as well as in other countries is tried to be provided with the help of some recent case studies.

Dockery *et al.* in their famous six U.S. cities study showed that mortality was more associated with the levels of fine, inhalabel and sulphate particles than with the total particulate concentration. In another study Dockery *et al.* estimated that for every increase of 10 microgram/m^3 R.P.M., the total mortality is raised by 1%. A more recent study in 20 U.S. Cities by Samet *et al.* in 2000 calculated that every 10 microgram/m^3 rise in R.P.M. increases total mortality by 0.51%. Romieu *et al.* study in Latin American countries showed that about 1% increment in total death is associated with every 0 microgram/m^3 increase in the respiratory particulate matter level (Green Governance, 2001).

According to estimates of the World Health Organization (WHO), more than one lakh people in India die due to Particulate pollution every year. A 1997 study by the Centre for Science and Environment (CSE), revealed that one person dies prematurely almost every hour in Delhi in 1995 due to only suspended particulate matter. Another study conducted by the World Bank revealed that premature deaths due to air pollution have gone up from 40000 in 1991-92 to 52000 in 1995 in Indian cities; an increase of 30% was recorded. A three year study by S.K. Chhabra of the Vallabbhai Chest Institute from 1996-98, found that (20-25) % of the adult population of Delhi was suffering from chronic respiratory symptoms like cough, breathlessness and wheezing. Rate of occurance of respiratory diseases in urban people were at least double than the people residing in the adjoining rural areas of Delhi. Another study conducted by the Chittaranjan national Cancer Institute and Environmental Biology Laboratory of the department fo Zoology of Kollkata University done between November 1997 and May 1999 revealed that about 43% of the Children in Kolkata are suffering from respiratory disorders compared to 14% among the rural children. Cough was present in 19% and allergic rhinitis (inflammation of the mucous membrane of the nose) in 10% of the urban children in comparision to 2-3 precent of the rural children respectively. Alarmingly, 94 to 96 percent of the children were found producing sputum, which would be reflective of habitual smokers. But only 5.5% of the children were found to be smokers and that too occasional. The main culprit was pollution in the ambient air with particulate pollution being the predominat factor (CSE, India).

6.0 Activities to Combat the Problem

In response to researches indicating that health effects were occuring even when the levels of particulate matter in the air were in compliance with the PM_{10} standard, indicating that fine particles ($PM_{2.5}$) are largely responsible for the health effects of greatest concern. United States Environmental Protection Agency (USEPA) published final revisions to its particulate matter standards in the month of July 1997 (the standard has last been revised in 1987). The revisions include the addition of a $PM_{2.5}$ standards. In addition, EPA indicated that the existing PM_{10} standards did not adequately protect visibility. EPA retained the original PM_{10} standard, revised the 24 hr. PM_{10} standard by changing its form to be more protective against the short-term exposure to coarse particles and added the following $PM_{2.5}$ standards. The new EPA standards were challanged in the court, in May of 1999. On 18th June 1999 the court ruled the that $PM_{2.5}$ standards should remain in place. The standards for $PM_{2.5}$ are shown in Table -1.

7.0 Conclusions

Among all the criteria air pollutants, the effect of the fine particulates ($PM_{2.5}$) on human health is most threatening. USEPA has taken steps to combat this $PM_{2.5}$ related hazards. They have incorporated $PM_{2.5}$ in their National Ambient Air Quality Standards (NAAQS). But as far as India is concerned, no stringent measures either in respect of control or standard has yet been adapted. Development and subsequent implementation of these standards will help millions of people in our country to enjoy a better quality of life.

It has been seen that there is a considerable increase in the respiratory disorders with a corresponding increase in the concent-ration of the particulate matters. Airborne manganese has been found to be associated with an increased probability for pneumonia in populations residing in the highly polluted industrial areas. Lastely the fine particulates, especially when it contain sulphate and nitrate act as the principal conveyor of acid in the atmosphere.

As far as India is concerned, a database of $PM_{2.5}$ also needs to be created. Mainly a chief alternative of filter paper to retain $PM_{2.5}$ is to be established. The cost is the basic constraint regarding the development of a proper data inventory of fine particulates. The first step for fine particulate matter control management is the creation of their data source. Again, the source apportionment of PM $_{2.5}$ is another important step for this management. Proper models are to be established to perform the cost benefit analysis of a control equipment for $PM_{2.5}$

Table 1 : For Fine Inhalable Particulates ($PM_{2.5}$) standards :

Avergeing Time	*Primary Standard*	*Secondary*
1-Year (new standard)	15 microgram/m³	15 microgram /m³
24-hr (new standard)	65 microgram/m³	65 microgram /m³

(Source : Reference No. 4)

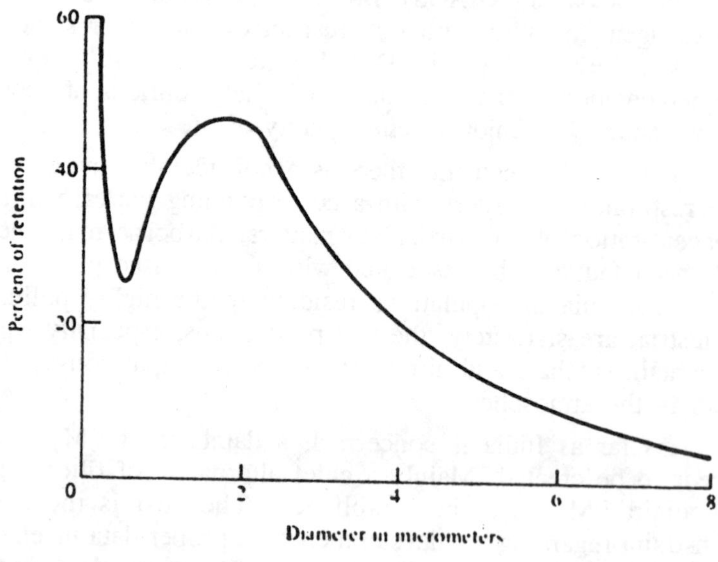

Fig. 7: Relation between size of particulate matter with percentage retention. (Source : Reference No. 5)

REFERENCES

1. http:// www.epa.gov/ttn/chief/ei data. html (Getting Started-$PM_{2.5}$ Emission Inventory)
2. "Green Governance", Newsletter, Vol II, Issue -III, West Bengal Pollution Control Board December 2001, Kolkata.
3. http : // www. cseindia.org/html/cmp/air/cng cngorder notel.htm.
4. EPS's Revised Particulate Matter Standards. html.
5. "Environmental Engineering" by Howard S.Peavy, Donald R.Rowe, George Tchnobanoglous, Mc Graw-Hill Book Company, International Edition 1985.
6. "Fine Particulate Pollution", A report of the United Nations for Europe, Pergamon Press.

10

Clean Car Standards

Vinod S.Patel

The clean Car Standard is a performance-based standard that is practically achievable by applying the best practices currently used by the global auto industry. The standard is intended to promote the near-term development of vehicles that are significantly greener than today's in their production, use and end-of-life disposition. Meeting these standards should complement other important values of praticality, affordability and safety. The standard includes the following components :

1. The Fuel efficiency improvement of 1.5 times the fleet average within that vehicle's class.
2. The Tailpipe emissions should meet California's "Super Ultra Low Emission Vehicle" (SULEV) standard.
3. The clean manufacturing practices that achieve superior environmental performance in the vehicle's manufacture and use of non-toxic recyclable materials.

1. Fuel Efficiency

Fuel efficiency improvements of 1.5 times the fleet average, within that vehicle's class. Improving fuel economy is fundamental to address many of the environemental problems associated with motor vehicles. A variety of options exist for improving fuel economy, ranging from numerous refinements in existing designs to advanced technologies that offer larger leaps forward in efficiency. Among the most existing recent developments in automotive engineering is the fact that some of these "leap forward" advanced technologies are ready for widerspread commerciali-zation. The resulting designs offer a 50% or higher improvement in fuel economy for a given size or style of vechicle without com-promising utility, safety, or performance.

Hybrid power trains combine the range and power of an internal combustion engine with the high efficiency of electric drive. Conventional auto engines are least efficient at low loads, whenever the vehicle is not accelerating rapidly or climbing a hill at freeway speeds. A hybrid power train allows the engine to be sized and tuned for higher efficiency under these common driving conditions, with an electric motor providing extra power from battery as needed to meet peak loads. Because a hybrid drive train has a battery (or other energy storage device) along with power electronics that manage motor and generator components connected to the wheels, it can also recapture braking energy that would otherwise be lost. This regenerative braking ability serves to further increase fuel efficency.

The worlds's first mass-produced hybrid vehicle is the Toyota Prius. It was Introduced to the Japanese market in December 1997. Prius reached sales of 18,000 in its first year on the market, with over 25,000 sold through the first half of 1999. The current Prius, which corresponds in size to a sub-compact car in the U.S. market, uses "Toyota Hybrid System" (THS) technology and a specially designed high-efficiency engine to achieve 66 mpg on Japanese driving cycles. U.S. driving cycles are more rigorous than those in Japan, and according to EPA tests, the Prius'49 mpg fuel economy is 66% better than the average subcompact on the U.S. market in 1998. Its fuel economy is 64% better than the average for its 3000 pound weight class. Toyota has announced that a version of the Prius is slated for U.S. sales in 2000. This model will be optimized for the U.S. market, and although its specifications are not yet public, it is expected to offer at least a 50% step forward in fuel economy over a comparable sized conventional car.

The next hybrid announced for mass prodcortion, and what may well be the first available in the United States, is the Honda Insight. It uses Honda's "Integrated Motor Assist" (IMA) techno-logy, which couples a highly efficient engine to an electric motor that draws additional power from a battery to boost both perfor-mance and efficiency. This two-seat sports coupe is targeted to achieve 70 mpg in U.S. driving cycles and meet California's ULEV emissions standard as well. Although final specifications have not been released, the Insight is expected to be similar in size too, but with better performance than the Honda CRX coupe that was sold through 1992. The standard engine version of Honda CRX was rated at 40 mpg, suggesting that the new Insight will offer a 75% fuel economy improvement over a similarly sized two-seater.

The Insight applies weight-saving aluminium structural technologies and aerodynamic styling as well as a hybrid drive train, all of which contribute to its substantial efficiency achievement. Even without a hybrid drive train, weight-saving and aerody-namic vehicle body designs can offer significant efficiency improvements. A number of automakers have shown prototype vehicles that use advanced, lightweight materials techniques to cut 40% or more from the weight of a given sized vehicle. Ford has done extensive development and testing on its aluminium-based P2000 platform, which is designed to achieve a 2000 pound curb weight in a mid-sized sedan (the average mid-size sedan now weighs about 3300 pounds). These models are designed to meet or exceed the crash worthyness of today's vehicles, so that safety is not compromised. By itself, a 40% weight reduction offers a 25% fuel economy improvement. A prototype P2000 using an advanced diesel engine was rated at 63 mpg, a 125% improvement over today's typical cars. Diesel pollution problems are yet to be solved, but using a state-of- the-art low-emission gasoline engine would allow an aluminium-based vehicle to easily exceed a 50% fuel economy improvement. In short, a number of advanced technology options now exists that can be applied to provide atleast a 50% boost in fuel economy while maintaining size, safety, performance and capacity and also meeting very low emissions standards (ULEV or better). Hybrid drive trains are one promising approach to achieving such efficiency improvement, but a similar degree of environmental excellence can also be attained with a lightweight, streamlined structure and an incrementally improved gasoline engine.

All of these technologies are applicable across the size spectrum of the car and light truck market. Thus, the Clean Car Campaign's specification of a 50% increase in fuel economy is a target that we expect any one of the major automakers could reach in the near-term.

2. Tailpipe Emissions

Tailpipe emissions meeting California's "Super Ultra Low Emission Vehicle" (SULEV) standard.

Even the cleanest and most efficient vehicle on the market today still pollutes the air and otherwise damages the environment. Motor vehicles emit several noxious pollutants. These vehicle emissions standards are designed to regulate:

* Hydrocarbons (HC) are volatile organic compounds that cause smog and are toxic and carcinogenic.
* Carbon monoxide (CO) is a poisonous gas that impairs the flow of oxygen to the brain and other parts of the body.
* Nitrogen oxides (NOx) aggravate respiratory problems, both directly and indirectly, by forming PM and smog; NOx also causes acid rain and damages aquatic environments.
* Fine airbone particualte matter (PM) causes lung trouble-shortness of breath, worsening of respiratory disease and heart conditions, lung damage, and cancer.

Currently, all new vehicles for sale in the United States (outside of California, New York, and Massachusetts) are certified to meet the Tier1 Federal emissions standard set by the U.S. Environmental Protection Agency (EPA). Tier 1 limits the amount of HC, CO, NOx, and PM coming from a vehicle's tailpipe and leaking from its fuel system. Vehicles sold in California, New York and Massachusetts must meet more stringent emission standards established by the California Air Resources Board (CARB) and adopted by the other two states.

To continue to improve air quality, tighter standards are needed nationally. CARB has already established stricter standards set to begin in model year 2004. Its Super Ultra-Low Emission Vehicles (SULEV) standard is the cleanest emission standard that a gasoline vehicle can meet. EPA has proposed a somewhat less stringent program—Federal Tier 2 standards— also set to begin in model year 2004. The Tier 2 proposal has an emissions standard almost identical to California's SULEV standard that auto makers could begin certifying to as early as MY 2001 SULEV represents to days's state-of-the-art in emissions control, and is a substantial leap forward compared to the current federal standard. The Clean Car Campaign has therefore adopted the SULEV standard.

The table below compares the SULEV standard to the current Federal Tier1 standard. It shows that to achieve the Clean Car Campaign-SULEV Standard, vehicle emissions must be reduced by 76 to 97 percent from current levels. This can be achieved through improved engine and catalytic-based control technologies, representing best practice for gasoline vehicle emissions currently available. By applying this standard to vehicles sold nationally, improvements in air quality can be achieved across the country. This Clean Car Standard also applies to both passanger cars and light-trucks.

A Comparison Of Emissions Standards

Pollutant	Clean Car Campaign-SULEV Standard (gram/*mile*)	Current Federal Standard-Tier (gram/*mile*	Reduction (Percent)
Hydrocarbons (HC)	0.01	0.31	97%
Carbon Monoxide (CO)	1.0	0.31	76%
Nitrous Oxides (NOx)	0.02	0.6	97%
Particulate Matter (PM)	0.01	0.10	90%

Notes :

- * Standards for light-duty trucks are less stringent in certain cases under Tier1 standards. The same Clean Car Campaign-SULEV Standard applies to both passanger cars and light-trucks.
- * Reductions based on a simple comparision of emissions standards for light-duty automobiles. SULEV standards are based on a 120,000 mile lifetime instead of 100,000 mile lifetime for Tier1 standards.
- * Achieving the full benefit of SULEV emission control technologies requires use of low-sulfur fuel, which is required in California but not yet available nation wide.

Neverthless, a vehicle that meets the SULEV standard still will be cleaner than average vehicle. Since most vehicles stay on the road for many years, its emission performance will improve as low-sulfur fuel is phased in strating of 2004, under its new fuel quality standards that EPA has proposed under Tier2.

Modern engine controls and improved catalyst design make these further emission reducations, one of the cheapest pollution control options available to the society. The technologies to reach the SULEV standard are further refinements to existing techno-logies. Achieving the full benfit of SULEV emissions control technologies, however, requires the use of low-sulfur fuel. At this time, low-sulfur gasoline is only required in California, and is not yet available nationwide. Nevertheless, substantial emssion benefits are expected form SULEV technology even when they are not fueled on relatively clean, lower sulfur gasoline. Furthermore, SULEV-certified vehicles outside of California will likely be able to take full advantage of their advanced control technologies when lower-sulfur gasoline is required nationally starting in 2004 as part of the EPA's proposed Tier 2 program. However, because the effects of sulfur can vary by design, we also are requesting to the manufactures to provide the campaign with data, to demonstrating substantial emissions reductions when operating with average nationwide gasoline.

3. Clean Manufacturing Practices

Achieves superior environmental performance in the vehicle's manufacutre and use of nontoxic recyclabe materials, to include:

a. Best-in-class painting/coating practices.

b. Elimination of heavy metals and other substances of concern.

c. Design for recyclability and maxium use of recycled materials

a. Best-in-class painting/coating practices:

A vehicle manufacturer must demonstrate auto body coating practices, which achieve the following level of VOC releases: 2 lbs. VOC/Vehicle.

Painting and coating of automobiles currently results in significant VOC emissions. It is also a highly energy intensive manufacturing process. Coating practices are a useful indicator of manufacturing "greenness" because they have important local health impacts and there is adequate publicly available data to base comparisons between facilities.

Our vehicle standard for coating practices has been developed by surveying the actual environmental performance of existing auto paint shops globally, as well evaluating the performance of emerging coatings technologies. For example, Diamler Chrysler has established an emission level of approximately 0.5 lbs per vehicle at its Rastatt, Germany plant using an integrated, water-based powder-slurry paint system. For US based plants, an emission of approximately 4 lbs per vehicle is achieved in practice using current technology.

The standard is currently set at a level (2 lbs. VOC/Vehicle), which is achievable in the near term, but also requires auto manu-factures to begin utilizing emerging coating technologies that result in significantly lower emissions. This level roughly corresponds to the newly proposed German paintaing coating standards, which is currently being achieved or exceeded at several German auto plants. The standard is expressed as Volatile Organic Compound (VOC) releases per vehicle in order to provide a standard, which can be used internationally.

b. Elimination of heavy metals and other substances of concern :

For a given vehicle, a manufacturer must track and report publicly on its progress in eliminating the following substances of concern, througout the vehicle's life cycle:

- — great lakes persistent toxic(glpt's)
- — lead
- — mercury
- — cadmium
- — hexavalent chromium
- — PVC
- — CFC's
- — persistent bioaccumulative substances (pbt's)
- — chlorinated solvents
- — asbestos

In addition, for the following components or processes where known and cost-effective alternatives are available, a manufacturer should demonstrate complete elimination of :

- — lead-free electrocoat (auto body anti-corrosion coatings)
- — mercury-free lighting/switches
- — PVC-free instrument panels, interiors, and undercoating-CFC- free cooling system
- — asbestos-free friction materials and engine gaskets

A number of substances of conern have been targeted for elimination or reduction by auto companies and govermments. For example, a voluntary agreement between automakers and the State of Michigan targeted 65 persistent toxic substances of concern to the great lakes. More reecntly, the European commission has targeted toxic heavy metals and PVC substances that are of concern of "End of Life Vehicles." In a Proposed Directive on environment friendly handling of End of Life Vehicles, the Commission has recommended phase-outs of lead, mercury, cadmium and hexav-alent chromium from such vehicles, with the possible addition of the plastic PVC. Other important international agreements have also targeted the phase-out of substances such as: CFC's, chlorinated solvents, and asbestos. Many companies are well on their way towards the eliminatin of such susbtances from their products and production processes.

In accordance with these international efforts, we have established a vehicle standard that requires the manufacturer to track and report publicly on its progress in eliminating substances of concern from manufacturing processes throughout a vehicle's life cycle. We also require complete elimination of such substances in cases where cost-effective alternatives are available.

c. Design for recyclability and maximum use of recycled materials :

Reusability or Recyclability :

A manufacturer must demonstrate that the vehicle is 80% by weight reusable or recyclable. Reusable means the part is customarily removed from the car before shredding and used as it is or remanufactured for reuse.

Recyclable means the material is customarily recycled before or after shredding by separating the material and reprocessing it into usable material for automotive or other applications. Com-bustion of a material for energy recovery is not considered recycling for purposes of this requirement.

Although a signifcant portion of the automobile (primarily the metal fraction) is now routinely resued or recycled, the sheer number of vechicles scraped results in about 2.5 to 3.0 million tons of auto shredder residue (ASR) being disposed of in solid waste landfills each year in the U.S. This residue often contains heavy meatals and other toxic chemicals, which can leach into plastics, rubber, fabric, and glass, represents a tremendous waste of resources. Faced with a shortage of landfill disposal capacity, several European countries, such as Sweden and the Netherlands, have mandated Extended Producer Responsibility. Toyota claims that it has already achieved 85% recyclability and plans to increase recyclability to 90% by 2000. General Motors has the goal of 90% recyclability by 2001, and Daimler Chryslers goal is 85% recylability by 2002. The European Commission has proposed a new directive, which will likely be adopted, which mandates minimum resuse and recycling percentages by certain German auto manufacturers, including U.S. companies, have agreed to an 85% goal by 2002. Based upon these agreements and goals in the automobile industry, and based upon the technical feasibility of increasing recycling, we have established the interim green vehicle standard of 80% reusability or recyclability.

Recycled Material Contents

The manufacturer must demonstrate that the vehicle contains the following levels of recyled content:

— 20% recycled contents for polymer parts

— 20% recycled contents for aluminium

— 30% recycled content for ferrous metals

For purposes of this requirement recycled content means a combination of post-industrial and post-consumer recycled material. The manufacturer must report on the percentage of recycled content, which is post-industrial versus post-consumer.

Using recycled materials in building automobile is an important means of closing the loop on automobile materials from end-of-life vehicles and also creates markets for recycling materials from other end-of-life products. Using recycled materials also reduce use of raw materials and energy and reduces pollution in the production of materials for automotive use. At leat two U.S. companies, Ford and Daimler Chrysler, have set public goals for recycled contents of materials used in building their cars. Diamler Chrysler, have set public goals for recycled content of materials used in building their cars. Daimler Chrysler, for instance, will require suppliers to provide 20% recycled content for plastic parts by 2000. The above-recycled content level are comparable to the requirements adopted by these companies.

Producer Responsibility

The manufacturer must demonstrate that it has a program for designing cars to enhance reuse and recycling and that it has produced a disassembly manual, which is available to dismantlers and automotive recyclers for the model in question.

Some form of producer responsibility for end-of-life vehicles will be necessary to increase reuse and recycling rates and improve the environmental performance of dismantlers and shredders. European Extended Producer Responsibility legislation and agreements have placed a financial responsibility on producers to ensure that the last owner can turn the vehicle over for reuse and recylcling without incurring any cost. In the United States the current level of reuse and recycling has been achieved through a market-based infrastructure, which accepts end-of-life vehicles typically without charged to the cast owner. whether higher levels of reuse and recycling and improved environmental performance of dismantlers and shredders can be achieved in the U.S. without jeopardizing the positive economic value of end of life vechicles has yet to be demonstrated. U.S. manufacturers have instituted programs for designing cars to enhance reuse and recycling and have conducted reseach programs to improve the dismantling of vehicles for reuse and recycling. The proposed European Union Directive would mandate that manfacturers have such programs and that they provide dismantling manuals for each car. These basic elements of producer responsibility form the basis for the standard for producer responsibility.

Sources :

1. California's "Super Ultra Low Emission Vehicle" (SULEV) standard
2. Toyota Car Manufacturer, Japan
3. Honda Car Manufacturer, Japan
4. U.S. Environmental Protection Agency (EPA)
5. California Air Resources Board (Carb)
6. General Motors, USA
7. European Commission (EC)
8. German auto manufacturers

11

Women And Quality of Life

Mona Mehta and Divya Ajwani

The world environment comes from the French Verb "Environner" which means to surround. In broad sense environment covers every conceivable thing on earth but operationally it is defined as "that bundle of resources which support, develop or enrich human life" (Doraiswamy, 1988). Environment is the sum of all social, biological or chemical factors which compose the surroundings of the man. Each element of these surroundings constitutes a resource on which man draws in order to develop a better life.

The physical environment includes not only the physical structures but also the related services and facillites (Parikh, 1980). It encompasses the non-living things and physical forces affecting man such as air, water, ventilation, illumination, temperature, sound, sanitation and so on.

Air Pollution is woven throughout the fabric of our modern life. A by product of the manner in which we build our cities, air pollution is the waste remaining from the ways we produce our goods, transport ourselves and our goods, generate energy to heat and light the place where we live, play and work and use fuels to cook the food we eat. The major cause of air pollution is combus-tion and combustion is essential to man.

Air Pollution has reached alarming levels in Indian metros. Delhi, Mumbai and Kolkata are three of the ten most polluted cities of the world. Due to multiple sources of pollution spread all over the city, no area is really safe and homes are affected with industrial smoke, vehicle exhaust, dust and gases in the air.

Women usually have to spend longer hours working in the house, therefore, they are worst affected by deprivations in respect of living conditions. This could affect their health and well-being (Swaminathan, 1985).

Man has been engaged in efforts to improve his standard of living from the very beginning of civlization. The inevitable outcome of this development and human evolution is the environmental pollution. It is axiomatic that the more advanced a civilization becomes the more complex are the problems related to man's environment namely, congestion, crime, housing, traffic, noise etc. it has become increasingly obvious that the improper disposal of solid, liquid and gaseous wastes is creating a burgeoning problem of environmental pollution. The resulting alteration of man's natural environment has reached a point where the environ-ment is now beginning to exert untoward effects on man.

Quality of life denotes the state of physical, mental and emotional health, civil rights, the performance of educational sytstem, the air, water, land and noise pollution. It also includes other dimensions such as adequte housing, enjoyment, healthy family to function according to changing times. Vermayen (1978) and Nair (1988) have reported that some of the measures or indicators of quality fo life are healthfulness of life, measurement of learning, time and leisure, employment, housing conditions, quality of natural environment, economic accessibility and so on.

Man has lived on earth exposed to various kinds of pollution for millions of years, probably because man has the ability to adapt himself to different environmental situations.

He has learnt to tolerate ugly surroundings, dirty skies, and polluted streams. Now, the sudden interest in checking pollution has arisen because the quality of man's life and his continued survival within limited environmental setting are reaching an alarming level and hence receiving national and international final attention. The rapid de-pletion of necessary resources and a progressive loss of the qualities that we identify with humanness and weakening of physical and mental sanity has forced us to consider the interdependence of man and his environment.

The immediate environment of man comprises of air on which depends all forms of life. Apart from supplying the life giving oxygen the atmospheric conditions serve several functions. The human body is cooled by the air contact. Air is rendered impure by respiration of man and animals, combustion of coal, gas, oil etc., decompositon of organic matter, trade and traffic and manufacturing processes which give off dust, fumes, vapours and gases.

Domestic pollution is not new. It dates back to the early cave man who discoverd this as an invaluable source of energy for keeping warm and cooking food but he had to flee out from time to time in order to escape the smoke and gases from the fire.

Certain features affect the environment in the kitchen. Among them are the various pollutants present in the indoor atmosphere of the kitchen as a result of combustion of various fuels for cooking. The WHO (1979) report indicated that indoor concentration of air pollutants are sometimes 50-100% higher then outdoor con-centrations. The indoor pollution prevails in the kitchen, which is the centre of food preparation. Since cooking is the most time consuming of the homemaker's tasks, who spends about 6-7 hours in a day in the kitchen. Thus it is essential to reduce her physical and mental drudgeries, which she faces while working in the kitchen. The heat generated by the different fuels is quite a hindrance in the efficiency of work.

The work level decreases as the domestic air pollution increases. Ill ventilaiton increases the temperature in the kitchen. If there is no proper outlet of heat and gases, the atmosphere becomes stuffy which reduces the efficiency of work. The indoor pollution not only affects the worker but indirectly the whole family.

An ill ventilated kitchen is dangerous for the homemaker. The temperature, moisture and stagnant atmosphere places, primarily diminish heat loss from the body, fall of blood pressure causing heart fatigue, un-stimulated nervous system and muscular tone, etc. Air polluted with smoke effect our health very much causing irritation of eyes, skin, mucus membrane and respiratory disorders.

Various pollutants found in the air are as follows :

Carbon Monooxide : A colourless, exceedingly faint metallic colour and taste, highly poisonus inducing asphyxia. It arises in large amounts from the complete and incomplete combustion of carbon fuels. It reacts with blood haemoglobin to produce carbo-oxyhaemoglobin, which reduces the effectiveness of oxygen carrier in the blood stream.

Oxides of Nitrogen : Nitrogen dioxide acts as an acute irritant and in equal consideration is more injurious than nitric oxide in combination with unburnt hydrocarbon. The oxides of nitrogen react in the presence of sunlight to form photochemical smog which is dangerous to human health by damaging the lungs and causing eye irritation.

Hydrocarbons : They do not appear to cause any appreciable corrosive damage to materials. Some cancers appear to be caused by exposure to aromatic hydrocarbons found in soot and tar. Methane has a very low photochemical activity.

Going through the various national and international journals of air-pollution it was found that very less work has been done on domestic pollution. An intensive study done by Yokum, Clink and Cote of Indoor and outdoor pollution found that the daytime concentrations of pollution were high as compared to night time concentrations. In contrast to particulate matter concentration the organic content of of particulate matter was enriched in the indoor samples, than the out door samples. This finding was attributed to smoking and cooking activities indoor.

According to a research paper presented in workshop by Siddiqui, Carpanter, Hufschuidst (1981) on the major sources of air pollution in cities of developing countries found that the pollutants were from insufficient combustion of home heating and coolking fuels and from old and improperly maintained vehicles.

The primary thrust is defining air quality and its relationship to human health effects has been directed at the outdoor ambient atmosphere, whereas, a large percentage of time is spent indoors, by an average person. The quality of indoor air differs from that of the outdoor air, it varies widely and can be influenced by various factors. Govt. of India document prepared for the United Nations in 1982 admitted that the persent total emission of carbon monooxide, carbon dioxide, sulphur dioxide, nitrogen dioxide, organic matter, etc., are much larger from burning of firewood, cattle dung, vegetable waste products and refuge, etc. This is mainly because half of all the energy consumed in India is for cooking purposes and over 90% is from the so-called non-commercial fuel sources.

Domestic pollution can be prevented by a number of measures. NGO's social workers, women activists and home scientists should spread awareness regarding environmental sanitation and quality through formal and informal programmes. Town planners should strictly implement proper zoning of land. Proper ventilation should be planned.

12

Studies on the Effect of SO_2 from Mathura Refinery on Medicinal Plant *Nyctanthes arbor-tristis* Linn.

R. B. Singh

The studies on the effect of sulphur dioxide produced from Mathura Refinery were observed on medicinal plants like *Nyctan-thes arbor-tristis* Linn. (Harsingar), It inhibits RUDP carboxylase activity absorbed by leaves. SO_2 goes into the plant alongwith precipitation affecting the leaves. The plants grown in vicinity of smelters and polluted area of Mathura Refinery noted necrosis of leaves, defoliation of young terminal branches, hardening of floral buds and necrosis of seed tips. It is also observed that the exposure of Harsingar plant by SO_2 resulted to peephytin by removing magnesium ions (Mg^{++}) from chloroplast. Thus, affecting the photosynthesis activity, SO_2 also led to plasmolysis in leaves of this plant to convert pollutants into ammonium sulphate.

Introduction

Nyctanthus arbor-tristis Linn. belongs to family-Oleaceae, Vern. Name Hindi: Harsingar, is a native of India occuring wild in the sub-Himalayan region from Chenab to Nepal upto 1500 m and in Chhota Nagpur, Rajasthan, Madhya Pradesh, and South West to Godavari. It is widely cultivated throughout India as a garden plant for its fragrent flowers and is a hardy large shrub upto 15-25 feet high with grey bark. It is an ornamental and medicinal plant. Leaves are opposite, ovate, accuminate, entire with a few large distant teeth, rough, scrabrous above densely pubsecent beneath. Leaves contained tannic acid, methyl salicylate, the ascorbic acid content increases on frying the leaves in oil. Leaves are antibiotic and expectorent and are useful in the Ayurvedic system of medicine for the treatment of a variety of diseases such as fever and rheumatism, sciatica and intestinal worm infection.[4] The leaves extracted juice is acrid and bitter and useful as cholagougue, laxative, diaphoretic and diuretic. It is given to childeren for the expulsion of round and thread worms.

Leaves of this plant reveals the presence of flovonal glycosides[5] astragalin (Kaempferol-3-glucoside) and nicotiflorin (Kaempferol-3-rahmnoglucoside), friedelin, lupeol and olecinolic acid with corresponding 3-4 seco acid, nycthant acid is of biogenetic significance. Since the seed polysaccharides are useful in various industries investigation deals with the effect of sulphur dioxide on medicinal plant of *N. arbor-tristis* Linn. Leaves causing a great damage to plant. The seed polysaccharides of this plant have already been studied[7-9] and detailed studies on the effect of SO_2 from Mathura Refinery is greatly needed.

Environmental pollution has long been recognized as a major threat to ecosystem. Now, it is receiving attention at national and international forums due to its numerous effects not only on climate, plants and animals but also on buildings and materials. Thousands of air pollutants originate from automobile exhaust (60%), industry (20-30%) and fossil fuels (10%). Moreover natural processes like forest fire, volcanic activities, lightening and biological decay are also responsible for air pollution which inhibit growth of plants.

Air pollution is largely confined to troposphere. The mesosphere generally remains unaffected. As we know that

SO_2 is most widely spread pollutant which originate from Mathura Refinery, but because of its high reactivity and short life in atmosphere. However, the SO_2 have been reported in all industrialized areas of Mathura Refinery.

In many countries the modified air quality standards are prescribed[10]. Now a days the SO_2 concentrations below 400 $\mu g/m^{-3}$ can be tolerated by plants and animals but concentrations above this limit should be restricted in accordance with empirical equation[11]. Which is (C-400)xT=1700sg/m³/hr.

Where; C=SO_2 Concentration ($\mu g/m^3$)
T=Exposure time (hrs.)

Method

For measuring the Sulphur dioxide concentration for a short period from one hour to one day and the modified method[12] incorporating sodium tetra chloro mercurate absorbing solution gives satisfactory and reproducible results[13]. The lead dioxide sulphation method[13] is used for a longer averaging periods from a week to one month. The estimation of SO_2 in surroudings of Mathura Refinery were studied, the sample collection vessels were each spiked with sodium tetrachloromerurate solution (2.5 M, 1ml) and analysed[12]. The data of (2001-2002) of SO_2 concentrations from hour to hour and season to season are listed in table below.

Table 1 : Four Hourly, Monthly average concentration of SO_2 ($\mu g/m^3$) for the year 2002.

Month	Hours				Hours			Daily	Daily
	6-10	10-14	14-18	Day time mean	18-22	22-02	02-06	Night time mean	Mean
January	24	15	18	19	20	35	18	25	22
February	14	12	25	17	33	27	12	24	21
March	12	10	26	16	32	13	11	22	19
April	19	32	18	23	24	14	25	21	22

May	18	20	19	19	30	18	15	21	20
June	20	20	41	27	51	40	29	40	34
July	81	72	63	72	78	64	92	78	75
August	73	59	72	68	96	84	78	86	77
September	34	11	24	23	24	24	18	22	23
October	35	11	26	24	25	26	18	23	24
November	36	12	27	25	27	28	17	24	25
December	31	19	49	33	26	34	36	32	33
Average	**33**	**25**	**34**	**31**	**39**	**34**	**39**	**35**	**33**

Results and Discussion :

Sulphur dioxide produced from Mathura Refinery produces gases like SO_2 which are further oxidised to SO_4 which on hydration gives H_2SO_4. The SO_2 is responsible for sulphurous smog called London smog or reducing atmosphere. About 80 million tons of SO_2 released is leased into atmosphere per year. The low concen-tration of these pollutants over long period leads to intraveinal chlorosis. In high humidiy the SO_2 combines with leaves to form an aerosol, which erodes cuticle and cell membrane, thus inviting easy entry of pathogens. It also inhibits RUDP carboxylase activity getting absorbed by leaves, SO_2 goes into the plants alongwith precipitation, altering thereby the pH of plant and affecting the leaves of the plant.

The dominant species are replaced by slow growing and under storey species in SO_2 polluted area. The plant of *N. arbor-tristis* is growing in vicinity of smelters, brick klins and Mathura Refinery noted necrosis of leaves, defoliation of young terminal branches, hardening of floral buds, necrosis of seed tips.

REFERENCES

1. Drury, C.H., The Useful Plants of India, 314(1991).
2. Gambile, J.S., Flora of Presisency of Madras, pub., Botanical Survey of India, 2:556(1967).
3. Deshaprabhu, S.B., The Wealth of India, Raw materials, CSIR pub., New Delhi, 7:69(1966).

4. Chopra, R.N., Nayar, S.L., and Chopra, I.C., Glossry of Indian Medicinal Plants, CSIR pub, New Delhi, 177 (1956).
5. Singh, S.P.; Bhattachari, S. and Neelakantan, S., Bull. Nat. Inst. Sci. India, 31:41 (1965).
6. Cheesman, W.L., Blood and Blood Plasma Substitue, US Dept. Agri, IC, Peoria 3:289(1950).
7. Singh, R.B. and Jindal V.K., J. Indian Chem. Soc. 62:627 (1985).
8. Singh, R.B. Polish J. Chem. 65:353(1991).
9. Singh, R.B. J. Chemtracks, 1(2): 116(1999).
10. Sabura, Y.J. Air Pollution Control Association, 23:945(1973).
11. Dresinger, M.F., Govern P.C. and Govern, N.C. Conference on Impact of Air pollution on Vegetation, Toronto, Canada, (1970).
12. West, P.W. and Gaeke, G.C. Anal. Chem., 29:1816(1956).
13. Scaringelli, F.P., Saltzman, B.E. and Frey, S.A., Anal. Chem., 39:1709(1967).
14. Zutshi, P.K., Mahaderan, T.N. Vaidyanathan, N. and Sathe, A.P. Ind. Environ. Health. 20:14(1978).

13

Assessment of Air Pollution Load And Its Effect on Jowar (*Sorghum vulgare*) Crop, Plant growth Performance and Soil Physico Chemical Characteristics

Navin K. Sharma

Present investigation deals with five localities, differences in kharif crop-Jawar plants growth performance, soil physico-chemical characters and air pollutant status. Agra atmosphere is supposed to be polluted due to local industries, transport and perhaps also due to Mathura Oil Refinery situated 56 kms north-west of Agra. In order to understand whether the crop fields in Agra district are affected by air pollution and possible fallout of the pollutants on plants and soil, a network of five localities were selected on the basis of geographical directions. Jowar in the farmers field was selected as phytometer and Taj Mahal has been considered as epicenter. Among the five localities maximum air pollution in terms of SO_2, NOx and SPM was obtained at Gwalior road and minimum at Dayalbagh. The ANOVA had shown large localities variabilities of 52.03 at Gwalior road and Tajganj besides this small difference of 4.6 was obtained at Bichpuri. Locality variability has shown a correlation between air pollution and soil physico-chemical characteristic of 9985506±931311 which was higher at Sikandra, it was denoted by df. 2.43 at 5% and 2.87 at 1%

(tab value) respectively. Locality Sikandra has shown max values of ANP being 2771 gm m^{-2}, BNP being 230 gm m^{-2} TNP being 3001 gm m^{-2}, max height of plants being 379.3 cms and max. length of roots being 36 cms. Analysis of variance of Kharif crop-Jowar plant analysis had shown significant values of plants height, number of plants and yield as the determining factor.

Keywords : ANP, BNP, TNP, Edaphic, Epicentre, Air Pollution load

Introduction

Ever since Goverment of India decided to setup Mathura oil refinery in 1973, some apprehensions were expressed about the possible adverse effects on the historical monuments in the Agra-Mathura region from the gaseous emissions to be discharged from the refinery. NEERI (1993) in their report has shown air pollution effects from local industries after that voice has been raised that air pollution load at Agra Taj Trapezium Zone is not only harming the importnat historial monuments like Taj Mahal, Fatehpur Sikri and others but is also adversely affecting the plant and animal lives as also human health....? As a result of this several expert committee were formed by Goverment of India, the last committe formed was headed by Varadarjan (1995) submitted report "Atmospheric environmental quality and preservation of Taj Mahal and Agra monuments". Hence the interest arised, whether the air pollution load is directly adversely affecting the sensitive crop plants in *in vitro* condition, extensive work has been done on air pollution effects of plants. Aamlid, and Kare (1993) worked on methods of monitoring effect of air pollution on forest and vegetation of easter finemark. Impact of O_3, and SO_2 on reproductive development in oil seed rape (*Brassica napus* L.) by Bosac (1994). Fowler, (1978) worked on dry deposition of SO_2 on agricultural crops. Present study was made to monitor the locality difference in relation to growth performance and correlate it with soil physico-chemical charcters and the possible impact of load of air pollution fall out thereon.

Results and Disccussion :

Table 1 : Status of air pollution-kharif crop

Localities	SPM	SO_2	NOx
Bichpuri	305.7	15.22	48.5
Dayalbagh	322.5	8.73	24.4
Sikandra	305.7	15.22	48.5
Tajganj	432.0	8.16	31.7
Gwalior road	522.2	21.77	70.4

SPM-Suspended particulate matter. all values in μgm^{-3}, SO_2-Sulphur dioxide, NOx-different oxides of nitrogen

Table 2 : ANOVA of air pollution kharif crop

Sources of variation	*df*	*Sum of square*	*Mean squares*	*SD variance*
Among the means of conditions	4	8673.71	2168.43	73.16±223.03
Within conditions	10	364431.63	36443.16	

df-degree of freedom, SD-Standard deviation

Reffering to table 1 and 2 considering the status of air pollution load large locality variation i.e. maximum at Gwalior road and minimum at Dayalbagh was obtained during kharif crop-Jawar. The analysis of variance of air pollution load in different localities interprets the growth dependent effects during kharif crop seasons. While ref to table 2 locality variability showed a correlation between air pollution and soil physico-chemical characteristics of 9985906±931311 which was higher at Sikandra, it was denoted by degree of freedom 2.43 at 5% and 2.87 at 1% (f tab value) respectively. The Anova has shown large localities variabilities of 52.03 was obtained at Gwalior road and Tajganj besides this small difference of 4.6 was found at Bichpuri regarding air pollution during kharif crop season.

Table3 : Growth performance of Kharif crop-Jawar plants

Localities	*ANP in gm m-2*	*BNP in gm m-2*	*TNP in gm m-2*	*Height of plants in cms*	*Number of plants*	*Length roots in cms*	*Yield q/ha*
Gwalior road	2311	145	2456	261	12	23.5	85.6
Tajganj	1489	152	1641	344.2	23	30.5	61.2
Sikandra	2771	230	3001	379.3	25	36	68
Bichpuri	1259	175	1434	262.2	14	31.2	85.8
Dayalbagh	2018	162	2180	308.4	41	27.6	25.9

ANP-aboveground net production, BNP-belowground net production, TNP-total net production.

The *kharif* crop (Jowar plant analysis) had shown large variation among the localities studied. Locality Sikandra had shown maximum values of ANP being 2771 gmm-2, BNP being 230 gmm-2, TNP being 3001 gmm-2, max height of plants being 379.3 cms and maximum length of roots being 36 cms. Locality Gwalior road had shown minimum values of BNP being 145 gmm-2, height of plants 261 cms, number of plants 12 and length of roots 23.5 cm. Locality Bichpuri had shown maximum values of ANP being 1259 gmm-2, TNP being 145 gmm-2, height of plants 261 cms, number of plants 12 and length of roots 23.5 cm. Locality Bichpuri had shown maximum values of ANP being 1259 gmm-2, TNP being 1434 gmm-2. While loacality Dayalbagh had shown maximum values of number of plants being 41 and minimum yield being 25.9q/ha.

Table 4 : Anova of growth performance of kharif crop-Jowar Plants

Characters	df	SS	MSS	F(Cal)	F(tab)	CF
ANP	4	1122762	280690.6	0.409624	2.642	16735056
	35	23983384	685239.5			
BNP	4	3833.38	958.345	0.1424	2.642	216823.2
	35	235382.3	6725.21			
TNP	4	1227847	306961.9	0.379879	2.642	20761628
	35	2828131	808052.3			

Plant	4	100349.5	25087.39	3.278309	2.642**	451673.6
height	35	267838.9	7652.539			
Number	4	105491.9	26372.97	7.788021	2.642**	259905.83
of Plants	35	118522.3	3386.351			
Yield	4	113103.6	29063.8	7.76213	2.642**	9986.7
	35	236554.2	4162.4			

ANP- above ground net production, BNP below ground, TNP total net production.

The analysis of variance of Kharif crop-Jowar plants analysis had shown significant values of plant height, number of plants and yield as the determining factor.

Table 5 : Kharif crop-Jowar Soil physico-chemical analysis

Localities	*Soil mois- ture*	*Soil pH*	*N in kg/ha*	*P in kg/ha*	*K in kg/ha*	*Organic Carbon in%*	*Na in kg/ha*	*Ca in kg/ha*
Dayalbagh	8.8	8.5	448.6	18.5	0.72	48.5	28	
Sikandra	13.59	8.6	328.7	14.6	154.30	0.66	68	18.7
Tajganj	14.8	8.6	252.8	16.8	131.10	0.48	53.2	19.2
Gwalior road 16.2	8.7	325.0	18.4	177.60		0.56	65	38.5
Bichpuri	9.8	8.6	336.8	15.3	178.80	0.54	48	25

Table 6 : Anova of Kharif Crop-Jowar showing Soil physico-chemical analysis

Characters	*df*	*SS*	*MSS*	*F(Cal)*	*F(tab)*	*CF*
Soil	4	670.2367	167.5592	1.920821	2.457	9600.561
Moisture	65	5670.151	87.23309			
Nitrogen	4	0.23878	0.059695	2.093133	2.457	6.523956
	65	1.853764	0.028519			
Potassium	4	70588.06	17647.01	5.416845	2.457**	1550794
	65	211757.2	3257.803			
Exchange-	4	6945.657	1736.414	19.65027	2.45**	45619.56

Table Contd.

Characters	*df*	*SS*	*MSS*	*F(Cal)*	*F(tab)*	*CF*
Calcium	65	5743.786	88.36593			
pH	4	200.2857	50.07143	3.264904	2.457**	18892.86
	65	1.889286	0.029066			
Phos-	4	200.2857	50.07143	3.264904	2.457**	18892.86
phorus	65	996.8571	15.336226			
Organic	4	0.569937	0.142484	1.77171	2.457	22.658
carbon	65	7.8677571	0.12104			

df- Degree of freedom. SS-Sum of squares, MSS-Mean square variance, CF-cumulative frequency

Ref. to table 5 & 6 locality Dayalbagh soil physico-chemical analysis had shown maximum values of nitrogen being 448.6 kg/ha, P being 18.5 kg/ha, K being 0.72% while minimum values of soil moisture being 8.8% and pH value of 8.5 was obtained. Locality Sikandra had shown maximum values of exchangeable Na being 68 kg/ha and minimum values of phosphorus 14.6 kg/ha and exchangeable Ca being 18.7 kg/ha. Tajganj had shown min. values of nitrogen being 252.8 kg/ha, Potassium being 108.1 kg/ha and organic carbon being 0.48% locality Gwalior road had shown max. values of soil mosture being 16.2%, soil pH of 8.7 and exchangeable Ca being 38.5 kg/ha, while locality Bichpuri has shown minimum values of 48 kg/ha. The fertility status determined by NPK maximum values was obtained at locality Dayalbagh being 645.9% kg/ha and minimum at Tajganj being 280.7 kg/ha.

The ANOVA of soil physico-chemical characters significant values of K, Ca, pH, P and Na were obtained. The correlation between the growth performance of plants and air pollution and soil physico-chemical characters and air pollution has shown negligible values of 995794 ± 99351 and results infutes Null hypothesis 39.37 (Non significant at 5%) thus obtained data shows large locality differences but with no particular sequence.

The air pollution load is directly not adversely affecting the Jowar crop plants and sensitive soil characteristics.

REFERENCES

Amalid, Dan and Kare Venn (1993) Methods of monitoring the effects of air pollution on forest and vegetation of eastern finnmark, Norway. *Nor. J. Agri. Sci.* 7(1) :71-87.

Bosac, C.J.A, Roberts, V.J. and C.R. Black (1994) Impact of O_3 and SO_2 on reproductive development in oil seed rape (*Brassica napus* L.) *New phytologist* 126 (1) : 71-79.

Brimblecombe, P. (1986) Air composition and chemistry, Cambridge university press, Cambridge.

Durham J.L. (1984) The chemistry of particles of fog and rain, John Willey & Sons, New York.

Flower, D.(1978) Dry deposition of SO_2 on agricultural crops. Atmos. Environ, 12,369.

Khanna, P., Agarwal, A.D. and Thakre (1993) "Air Pollution studies to redefine Tan Trapezium Cordinates" report submitted to ministry of environment and forests, Government of India by National Environmental Engineering Research Institute, Nagpur.

Mishra, R, (1968) Ecology work book.

Pandya, S.C., Puri, G.S. and J.S. Singh (1968) Research methods in plant ecology. Asia publishing house, New Delhi.

Uttar Pradesh Gazetter Repro. (1965) Agra district, U.P. Govt. Press, Lucknow.

Vardarajan, S. (1995) "Atmospheric environmental quality and preservation of Taj Mahal and Agra monuments". Report submitted to Ministry of Environment, Goverment of India.

14

Sprawling Sayaji Park : Importance in the Present Scenario

K.N. Thaker and Y.T. Jasrai

Advancement and development leave great impacts on different organisms where man is not an exception. He is snatched out from all the essential conditions and now conditioned to smell of petrol fumes. Today man in large town leads a crumpled and unhappy life. Now a days man's attitude towards the preservation and protection of the environment has greatly changed which leads them to make gardens and parks. Gardens aim to be source of aesthetic and intellectual delight. They are the proud part of the national heritage (Randhawa, 1971). Gardens help in reducing the miserable shabbiness of the town or city. In Indian culture, parks and gardens have an important role in enjoyment of life. In 19th century (1875-76) Gaikawadi State of Vadodara planned to develop a well maintained garden, which could fulfill aesthetic pleasure of the citizens of Vadodara. Sayaji Park is situated within the built up area of Vadodara city, and holds a special place in the hearts of its citizens. In 1875, plan of Garden was worked out under the leadership of Colonel Carls. For the garden, land near Fatehgunj was chosen. The garden plan was implemented by an engineer, Fone Stumph, who was trained in Austria. The garden was put open for the common people of Vadodara on 4th January 1875. The sprawling vegetation including trees, number of seasonal ornamentals, shrubs and climbers are very striking features of the land surface. They prevent the degradation of physical features of the earth. They help in maintaining the ecological balance of nature. The vegetation helps in reducing the temperature, scavenging the air pollution and provides shelter to birds and animals besides supplementing fruits and other produces. Though Sayaji Park is not a Botanical Garden, it shows great diversity of species. It cannot be considered inferior to any Botanical garden. It represents best example for *ex situ* conservation.

Introduction

With rapid scientific and technological advances just underway, we hardly gave a thought to the possible consequences of the intensive exploitation of natural resourses. We were too busy to think of the fate of the biosphere—the outer cover of the planet which reflected all the consequences of our economic activities. The biological resources though seemed to be unlimited the exploitation is not sustainable. However, due to the extreme consequences of our attitude towards the preservation and protection of the environment has greatly changed now.

We always crave for beauty. This desire for beauty is also a race heritage, because people have enough to eat, space to live and keep them happy (Jindal, 1970). So they started seeking beauty. This desire leads them to making of gardens. Gardens aim to be source of aesthetic and intellectual delight (Randhawa, 1965). They are the proud part of the national heritage. Gardens help in reducing the,miserable shabbiness of the dwellings in town or city.

History of Sayaji Park

Sayaji park situated within the built up area of Vadodara city, and holds a special place in the hearts of its numerous admirers. In Indian culture, parks and gardens have an important role in day to day life according to tradition. In 19th century (1875-76) Gaikwad State of Vadodara planned to develop a well maintained park and garden which could fulfill aesthetic pleasure for the citizens of Vadodara.

In 1875, plan of the Garden was worked out under the

leadership of Colonel Carls. For this garden a land near Fatehgung was chosen. Formerly this area consisted of many *Shivalayas,* farms and tree avenues. The state acquired these *farmlands* of 87 acres. The garden plan was implemented by an engineer Fone Stumph who was trained in Austria. The main inspiration for this garden was European Gardens of that era.

The garden was put open for the citizens of Vadodara on 4th January 1876. The inauguration was coincided with the ceremony of laying the foundation stone of the Baroda College. The first Director of the garden was Sir John M. Henry, who had earlier worked at Kew Botanical Garden, London. During his tenure floral diversity in the garden was planned and developed. He brought many seeds and seedlings from various forests and from other countries. Sir Henry brought 40 Palmyra palms from Navsari. The Maharaja also brought saplings of *Hyphaene dichotoma* the only branched palm endemic to Gujarat, Westren Indian date palms and some flowering climbers from Kodinar region. Different varieties of banana and grapes were also brought from California. Elephant Bamboo *(Ochlundra fravonceria)* from Travancore and *Vanila* were brought from Chennai. An Ambavadi was also prepared which was a good source of income for the garden. For further development of the garden more area was acquired by the garden authorities.

Now the total land area of the garden is **113** acres, covering green landscapes, different tree species and zigzag passage of the river Vishwamitri which runs through. The garden is frequented by early risers (during morning hours), general public, visitors and tourists throughout the day. The garden has a marked influence on the children activities as it houses several centers of attractions (Table-1). During cool hours of evenings the garden get packed up with large number of families with their guests and children.

Table-1: Centers of attraction in Sayaji Park

1. Floral clock
2. Band Stand

3. Toy train
4. Zoo including aviary
5. Planetarium
6. Museum
7. Children traffic park
8. Play ground

The park is located in the heart of the modern city of Vadoadara and is like an efficient lung which purifies the ever fuming polluted air because of its sprawling plant wealth spread throughout the 113 acres of its land. It is more so important because it is located very near to the railway and bus stations which have the *meeting* point of all the roads ramifying the whole city.

Sayajipark is one of the most carefully planned gardens. The garden has been divided into several partitions covered with thick carpet of lawns, beautified with seasonal ornamentals, climbers, trees and also demarcated with well maintained hedges of *Clerodendron inermis, Thunbergia lauriformis,* and *Ipomea digitata.*

During our survey we have listed 97 tree species (Table-2). These tree species seemed to have been chosen with due regards to the colour of flowers, the beauty of foliage and shape of the crown. Most of them have been brought from tropical South East Asia. All of them have adapted this environment very well and growing successfully creating an illusion of age.

There are many trees in the garden which are rare *(Sterculia alata, S. foetida, Tecomella undulata),* endemic *(Hyphaene dichotoma)* and some are quite uncommon *(Cinnamomum camphora, Diospyros embryopteris, Ehretia laevis, Ficus benjamina, Crescentia cujete).* Varied tree forms with reference to branching pattern, roots, fruits, leaves etc. have been selected for not only their presentation but also for beautiful effects that have been created by planting them in groups *(Mangifera indica, Kigelia pinnata, Parkia biglandulosa).*

The garden is lined up with well-developed tared roads for pedestrians. At both the sides of roads a multiple rows of trees with foliage *(Polyalthia longifolia, Melia azaderach, Azadirachta indica)* have been planted so that in hot summer these trees provide a refreshing shade.

While some species which flowers at the same time (Fig.1) like *Bombax ceiba, Delonix regia, Spethodea campanulata, Tebebuia argentea, Couroupita guianensis* and *Peltophorum pterocarpum* are planted side by side really gives a colourful display when they are in full bloom. The royal palms *(Roystenia regia)* standing in the green lawns and shooting towards the sky with scanty crown creats a beautiful view near band-stand. This section is the heart of garden and is the best place for gathering.

The green domes of *Ficus benghalensis, Ficus religiosa, Tamarindus indica* planted at several points give a touch of countryside. In the interior, where the shape of the crown is not so important, trees with beautiful flowers and foliage *(Cassia fistula, Bauhinia variegata,* different *Cassia* (Fig.2), *Lagrstroemia speciosa, Alstonia scholaris,* and *Callistemon lanceolatus)* add to the scenic beauty. The groves of Kadamba *(Anthocephalus indicus, Haldinia cordifoba)* and shivlingi *(Couroupita guianensis)* form a nesting place for many birds like cattle egrets, crow feasant, etc. Birds and mammals relish their flowers and fruits and they play important role in pollination and dispersal of the seeds of these plants. Sayajipark has also exclusive collection of some seasonal ornamentals, woody shrubs and climbers (Table. 3). Ornamentals including varions varieties of *Canna* create beautiful world of colour with changing seasons.

Other than these vast collections of plants Sayaji Park has other attractions like Planetarium, Floral clock, Museum with a striking landscape with splendid architecture is a conspicuous reminder of the Gardens of 19th century. The museum has excellent collection on Indian history, cultures, customs, arts and crafts.

Sayajipark as a source of aesthetic and intellectual delight has become a proud part of Baroda city. Moreover, it helps in changing the concrete landscape of the city, maintaining the ecological balance of the atmosphere and scavenging the air pollution. Sayajipark with a sprawling landscape showing a great diversity of groups and representing the best example for *ex-situ* conservation in fact, needs to be upgraded to the status of Sayaji Botanical Garden and Park.

Table-2 Tree diversity of Sayaji Park

1) *Acacia auriculiformis*
2) *Acacia nilotica* Linn.
3) *Achras sapota* Linn.
4) *Alstonia scholaris* Linn.
5) *Annona squamosa* Linn.
6) *Anogeissus sp.* Wall.
7) *Anthocephalus indicus* Rich.
8) *Azadirachta indica* Juss.
9) *Bauhinia variegata* Linn.
10) *Bombax ceiba* Linn.
11) *Borassus flabellifer* Linn.
12) *Butea monosperma* (Lamk.) Taub.
13) *Callistemon lanceolatus* D.C.
14) *Caryota urens* Linn.
15) *Cassia fistula* Linn.
16) *Cassia roxburghii* D.C.
17) *Cassia siamea* Lamk.
18) *Casuarina equisetifolia* (Linn.) Forst.
19) *Ceiba pentandra* (L.) Gaertn.
20) *Cinnamomum camphora* Linn.
21) *Cocos nucifera* Linn.
22) *Cordia dichotoma* Forst.f Prodr.
23) *Cordia sebestena* Linn.

24) *Couroupita guianensis* Aubl.
25) *Crataeva nurvala* Buch. —Ham.
26) *Crescentia cujete* Linn.
27) *Cycas revoluta* Thunb.
28) *Cycas rumphii* Miq.
29) *Delonix regia* Boj (W. Hook) Raf
30) *Diospyros embryopteris* Pers.
31) *Diospyros montana* Roxb.
32) *Ehretia laevis* Roxb.
33) *Emblica officinalis* Gaertn.
34) *Erythrina indica* Linn.
35) *Ficus benghalensis* Linn.
36) *Ficus benjamina* willd.
37) *Ficus glomerata* Roxb.
38) *Ficus hispida* Linn.
39) *Ficus krishnae* (C.DC.) Corner
40) *Ficus religiosa* Linn.
41) *Gardenia jasminoides* Ellis.
42) *Gauzuma ulmifolia* Lamk.
43) *Gmelina arborea* Roxb.
44) *Haldinia cordifolia* (Roxb.) Ridsdale
45) *Haplophragma adenophyllum* (Wall.) *P. Dop*.
46) *Holoptelea integrifolia* (Roxb.) Planch.
47) *Hyphaene dichotoma* (White) Furtado
48) *Ixora arborea* Roxb. ex Smith
49) *Kigelia pinnata* (Jacq.) D.C.
50) *Lagrstroemia speciosa* Pers.
51) *Lannea coromandelica* (Houtt.) Merrill
52) *Limonia acidissima* Linn.

53) *Madhuca longifolia* J.F. Gemel

54) *Mangifera indica* Linn.

55) *Manilkara hexandra* Linn.

56) *Melia azaderach* Linn.

57) *Melia composita* willd.

58) *Mimusops elengi* Linn.

59) *Mitragyna parvifolia* (Roxb.) Korth.

60) *Morinda tomentosa* Roxb.

61) *Murraya exotica* Linn.

62) *Pandanus odoratissimus* Linn. F.

63) *Parkia biglandulosa* W.& A.

64) *Parkinsonia aculeate* Linn.

65) *Peltophorum pterocarpum* (D.C.) Baker ex Heyne

66) *Pithecellobium dulce* (Roxb.) Benth

67) *Plumeria acutifolia* Poir. Seem.

68) *Plumeria rubra* Linn.

69) *Polyalthia longifolia* Bth. & Hk. f

70) *Pongamia pinnata* (Linn.) Pierre

71) *Derris macrocarpa Thoth.*

72) *Psidium guajava* Linn.

73) *Pterospermum acerifolium* Willd.

74) *Putranjiva roxburghii* Wall.

75) *Putranjiva venusta (Wight) Pax. & Hoffm.*

76) *Ravenala madagascarensis* Sonn.

77) *Roystonia regia* (H.B. & K.) O.F. Cook

78) *Samanea saman* (Jacq.) Merrill

79) *Santalum album* Linn.

80) *Sapindus emarginatus* Vehl.

81) *Sapium insigne* Trim.

82) *Saraca indica* Linn.

83) *Spathodea campanulata* Beauv.

84) *Sterculia alata* Roxb.

85) *Sterculia foetida Linn.*

86) *Streblus asper* Lour.

87) *Syzygium cumini* (Linn.) Skeels

88) *Tebebuia argentea* Linn.

89) *Tabebuia rosea* D.C.

90) *Tamarindus indica* Linn.

91) *Tecomella undulata* (Sm.)

92) *Terminalia bellerica* (Gaertn) Roxb.

93) *Terminalia catappa* Linn.

94) *Thespesia populnea* (L.) Soland. *ex* Correa

95) *Wrightia arborea* (Dennst.) Mabberly

96) *Wrightia tinctoria* R. Br.

97) *Zizyphus mauritiana* Lamk.

Table-3 List of herbs, shrubs and climbers in Sayaji Park

Herbs

1) *Acalypha wilkesiana*

2) *A. hispida*

3) *Alcea rosea*

4) *Aralia elata*

5) *Asparagus densifloris*

6) *Bowkeria gerrardiana*

7) *Calendula officinalis*

8) *Canna generalis*

9) *Celosia crestata*

10) *Chrysanthemum morilifolium*

11) *Codiaeum verigatum*

12) *Coleus blumei*
13) *C.rehneltianus*
14) *Cordyline terminalis*
15) *Cypruss alternifolious*
16) *Dahalia pinnata*
17) *Dianthus carryophylis*
18) *D. chinensis*
19) *D. barbatus*
20) *Dracaena fragrans*
21) *Euphorbia lectea*
22) *Gallardia grandiflora*
23) *Gazania nivea*
24) G. *regens*
25) G. *uniflora*
26) *Gerbera jamensonii*
27) *Helianthus latifolius*
28) *Lantana camera*
29) *Leuzeu cebtauroides*
30) *Lychnis slilene*
31) *Papaver nudicaule*
32) *P. orientale*
33) *Petunia hybrida*
34) *Philodendron pertusum*
35) *Pleome reflaxa*
36) *Salvia maxicana*
37) *Sensiverea trifaciata*
38) *Senecio cineraria*
39) *Solidago canadensis*
40) *Syngonium podophylum*

41) *Verbena tenera*

42) *Vinca rosea*

Shrubs

1) *Caesalpinia pulicherrima*

2) *Clerodendron inermis*

3) *Mundulea recemosus*

4) *Dombea elegans*

5) *Euphorbia pulcherrima*

6) *E. esculanta*

7) *Hemelia patins*

8) *Hibiscus rosa-chinensis*

9) *H. schizopatelous*

10) *H. brevipedunculata*

11) *Ixora macrothyrsa*

12) *Manihot esculanta*

13) *Murraya exotica*

14) *Mussaenda erythryphylla*

15) *M. philippica*

16) *Neriun oleander*

17) *Rosa polyantha*

18) *R. floribunda*

19) *R. odorata*

20) *Tabernaemontana corymbosa*

21) *T. divaricata*

22) *Thevetia peruviana*

Climbers

1) *Bignonia unguis-cati*

2) *Ipomea digitata*

3) *Pyrostegia venusta*

4) *Thunbergia lauriformis*

5) *Quisqualis indica*

REFERENCES

1) Jindal, S.L. (1970) Flowering Shrubs of India, CSIR Publication Division, New Delhi.

2) Randhawa, M.S. (1965) Flowering Trees, National Book Trust, New Delhi.

3) Randhawa, M.S. (1971). Beautiful Gardens, Indian Council of Agricultural Resarch, New Delhi.

Article 14

Pl. 1.Flowering plants of Sayaji Park in full bloom

a Spathodea campanulata Beauv.

b Couroupita guianensis Aubl.

c Bombax ceiba Linn.

d Tebebuia argentea D.C.

Pl. 2.a Bauhinia variegata Linn.

b Cassia fistula Linn.

c Cassia renigera Lamk

d Cassia roxburghii D.C.

15

Air Pollution And Its Impact: Some Reflections

Bindoo Bhatt and Jogender Singh

The main objective of development is to meet the specific needs of the people and to enhance their standard of life. Such enhancement is not attained merely by provision for more and more goods but has to improve the quality of life of people. In this context, utilization of natural resources through application of Science and Technology is done. In the process of this effort environment is being put a side.

Introduction

Rapid Urbanization and Industrialization has added to various such side effects. Air pollution amongest it needs to be addressed. Air pollution has become aweful ecological-medico problems. Vehicular emissions have been increasing adding to the air pollution problems.

This paper addresses magnitude of air pollution in general and its impact on health in particular. The paper also comes out with proper action plan to correct this problem.

1.1 The Concept

Rising industiral and urban development leads to increase in prosperity as measured by Gross Domestic Production (GDP), but with this increase there is generally a strong correlation with the other meaning of GDP-Garbage, Dust and Pollution.

Since the onest of the Industrial Revolution, there has been a steady change in the composition of the atmosphere. Thus 19th century saw the begining of air pollution in Europe on large scale.

One of the formal definitions of air pollution is "The presence of one or more contaminants in the atmosphere in such quality and for such duration as is injurious or tend to be injurious to human health or welfare, animal or plant life. It is the contamination of air by the discharge of harmful substances. This consists of gaseous pollutants, odour, Suspended Particulate Matter (SPM) such as dust, fumes, mist and smoke, causing severe problems to the surrounding. Energy generation, transportation and industries that use energy sources, are the major sources of human created air pollutiion. Thus, depending on their sources and interactions with other components of air, these pollutants can have different chemical composition and various impacts including health."

Air Pollution therfore is a major concern today as local activities lead to local problems and also national global consequences lasting for hours to decades (like global warming, ozone destruction, acid rains and transboundary smoke transport). Thus, it is a major environmental problem affecting the developed and developing countries.

1.2 Magnitude

London fog of 1952, which affected large number of people (and over 4000 deaths) was the first incident that made us aware of the damage done to atmosphere in process of economic development-industrialization. Again in December 1991(40 years later) another similar incidence took placet there. At this time it was automobile emission that were trapped into atmosphere. During this unusual episode there was increase in mortality by 10% and cardiovascular diseases by 14%. For elderly hospitable admission it increased by 19% and 43% for obstructive lung disease. The pollutants that are inhaled have serious impact on human health affecting lungs and respiratory system; but are also taken up by the blood and pumped all round the body. Of course, the effects of air pollution on human health are very complex as there are many different sources and their individual effects vary form one to another. The gases mentioned below are mainly out door pollutants.

1.3 Listed below are the major air pollutants and their sources

Carbon Monoxides (CO) :

Is a colourless, odourless gas that is produced by incomplete burning of carbon-based fuels including petrol, diesel, and wood. It is also produced form the combusition of natural and synthetic products such as cigarettes. It lowers the amount of oxygen that enters our blood. It can slow our reflexes and make us confused and sleeply.

Carbon dioxide (CO_2) :

Is the principle greenhouse gas emitted as a result of human activities such as the burning of coal, oil, and natural gases.

Chloroflorocarbons (CFCs) :

Are gases that are released mainly from air-conditioning systems and refrigeration. When released into the air, CFCs rise to the stratosphere, where they come in contact with few other gases, which leads to a reduction of the ozone layer that protects the earth from the harmful ultraviolet rays of the sun.

Lead :

Is present in petrol, diesel, lead batteries, paints, hair dye products, etc. Lead affects children in particular. It can cause nervous system damage and digestive problems and, in some cases, cause cancer.

Ozone :

Occurs naturally in the upper layers of the atmosphere. This important gas shields the earth from the harmful ultraviolet rays of the sun. However, at the ground level, it is a pollutant with highly toxic effects. Vehicles and industries are the major source of ground-level ozone emissions. Ozone makes our eyes itch, burn, and water. It lowers our resistance to cold and pneumonia.

Nitrogen Oxide (NOx) :

Consists of solids in the air in the form of smoke, dust and vapour that can remain suspended for extended periods and is also the main source of haze which reduces visibility. The finer of these particles, when breathed it can lodge in our lungs and cause lung damage and respiratory problems.

Sulphur dioxide (SO_2) :

Is a gas produced from burning coal, mainly in thermal power plants. Some industrial processes such as production of paper and smelting of metals, produce sulphur dioxide. It is a major contributor to smog and acid rain. Sulphur dioxide can lead to lung diseases.

1.4 Air Pollution and Health Impacts

During last two decades many scientific studies have documented the links between air pollution and human health. Pollutants such as PM10 and less than 2.5 microns, nitrogen oxides, sulphates,ozone, and acid aerosals have been found to be associated with deaths, asthma, cardiovascular and respiratory disease.

An assessment of health damage from exposure to high level of particulates in 126 cities world wide (annual mean level exceed 50μg/cubic meter), that these damages may amount to near 130,000 premature deaths, over 500,000 new cases of chronic bronchitis and many more lesser health effects. Globally some 50% of cases of chronic respiratory illness are now thought to be associated with air pollution.

A study was conducted in 1986-92 in Barcelona, Helinski, Paris and London(1982-1992) showed significant increase in number of reported cases of asthma. A World Bank study states that in Delhi one out of ten children aged 5-16 years suffer from Bronchial asthma.

Motor vehicles continues to be the most significant contribution to air pollution in most developing countries. Depending upon levels of motorization, density and type of industry, the sources of emission between cities of developed and develping coutries varies. For example diesel autorikshaws are more common in developing countries rather than in developed countries.

A blue sky is a rare scene in many major Indian cities. The thick pall that hangs ove them is the consequences, primarily of the heterogenous mix of our capital is classified as one of 10 most polluted cities in world, and levels in other cities are alarming.

The Published data of motor vehicles in major cities are as follows :

Table 1.1 : Details of vehicles registered in major cities include

Urban agglo-mera-tion district	*Two-whee-lers*	*Autos/ tempos*	*Cars/ cabs*	*Buses*	*Goods carri-*	*Tractors/ others*	*Total*
Agra district							
01.04.1985	47364	589	4056	241	4572	10382	68104
01.04.1990	102669	2195	7272	566	n.a.	17141	n.a.
01.04.1995	157547	4227	12328	1081	n.a.	24214	n.a.
01.04.2002	267272	8541	23574	1303	9368	29385	339453
Ahmedabad district							
01.04.1985	152493	22632	31891	15023	21970	22020	266029
01.04.1990	320906	37267	55371	17020	24348	29171	484083
01.04.1995	514615	42264	87331	21157	36397	42695	744459
01.04.2002	932991	68064	168833	22106	46138	67137	130569
Banglore U & R districts							
01.04.1985	195210	12375	58971	3812	12217	5881	288466
01.04.1990	415854	15754	85037	4243	18298	6555	545741
01.04.1995	594639	34335	120103	6454	24625	14220	794376
01.04.2002	1183752	64520	259001	10077	49037	30171	1596558
Bhopal district							
01.04.1985	95621	4931	16513	1425	2849	2365	123704
01.04.1990	126891	6582	19206	1837	3594	2798	160908
01.04.1995	189201	8467	24481	2300	4321	3255	232025
01.04.2002	263737	12586	30835	2898	5500	13255	328811

Urban agglo-mera-tion district	*Two-whee-lers*	*Autos/ tempos*	*Cars/ cabs*	*Buses*	*Goods carri-aages*	*Tractors/ others*	*Total*
Chennai UA (Chennai & Chengalpattu)							
01.04.1985	122123	6115	55529	2945	12337	798	199847
01.04.1990	338486	5580	113783	3657	28917	1871	492294
01.04.1995	565451	20849	148856	4317	23475	1460	76448
01.04.2002	988630	4771	250080	4541	31459	6202	1325683
Delhi state and union territory							
01.04.1985	579064	30017	166263	13522	52370		841236
01.04.1990	1113236	58934	354810	17844	92778		1637602
01.04.1995	1617732	58934	354810	177844	92778		2432295
01.04.2002	2265955	86985	989522	47578	161650		3551690
Faridabad district							
01.04.1985	18042	436	1396	65	1312	1267	22518
01.04.1990	54719	1288	1655	140	2178	6293	66273
01.04.1995	95702	5059	18860	869	62984	4809	188283
01.04.2002	99983	8738	23265	1183	69249	6563	208981
Greater Mumbai UA (Greater Mumbai & Thane districts)							
01.04.1985	167338	32351	236186	22506	46840	3427	508648
01.04.1990	305099	41814	302122	10878	75405	3623	738941
01.04.1995	434802	101597	313537	16291	83571	6070	955814
01.04.2002	787527	212862	547224	20718	124718	8215	1701264
Hyderabad & Reddy district							
01.04.1985	153799	11524	36134	1746	16354	941	220498
01.04.1990	420089	17954	51488	3318	24451	470	517771
01.04.1995	732491	22544	78017	4707	31974	1749	871483
01.04.2002	1153681	73785	177012	5318	50050	7118	1466984
Indore district							
01.04.1985	72449	6251	8632	2070	10023	4100	103625
01.04.1990	145226	6985	17363	2211	13931	5867	191583
01.04.1995	219578	8242	26442	4231	20511	9721	288725
01.04.2002	425114	11993	7542	12751	28250	24743	550393

Urban agglo-mera-tion district	*Two-whee-lers*	*Autos/ tempos*	*Cars/ cabs*	*Buses*	*Goods carri-ages*	*Tractors/ others*	*Total*
Jabalpur district							
01.04.1985	42804	518	4681	1034	4064	2178	55279
01.04.1990	98336	591	6888	1070	4420	2882	114187
01.04.1995	140510	1419	8209	1349	4907	4905	161299
01.04.2002	280567	2184	12202	4232	10812	9888	319888
Jaipur district							
01.04.1984	76550	3180	12448	6006	18037	6407	122628
01.04.1989	162278	4505	20860	8159	23468	9064	228334
01.04.1994	271827	5567	30471	11227	32530	13412	365034
01.04.2001	480570	9669	62231	14963	51606	21691	640730
Kanpur Nagar and village district							
01.04.1985	71853	1826	8769	586	8133	3156	94323
01.04.1990	135423	2212	10516			3574	
01.04.1995	190484		16303			4039	
01.04.2002	323699	4648	46024	1464	18064	4729	398628
Kochi (Ernakulam district)							
01.04.1985	25118	4872	17676	1575	4274	1109	54624
01.04.1990	66100	7050	23531	2958	6749	1340	107728
01.04.1995	165250	17012	37481	5176	15315	1547	241781
01.04.2002	253745	27572	71825	10048	37245	2703	403138
Kakjata UA (Kolkata, Howrah, 24 Parganas-South & 24 Parganas-north district)							
01.04.1985	160556	4968	177736	15736	62514	10375	431885
01.04.1990	217304	7100	219079	18330	75083	11480	548376
01.04.1995	294110	10146	270039	21352	90179	12703	698529
01.04.2002	467756	27003	380079	28923	105687	28003	1037451
Lucknow district							
01.04.1985	61018	1784	5000	1313	6208	3586	78909
01.04.1990	154786	3522		1948	7485	4725	172466
01.04.1995	226356	7156		2306	9616	9225	254559
01.04.2002	438897	7768	63192	3096	11731	14096	538780

Urban agglomeration district	*Two-wheelers*	*Autos/ tempos*	*Cars/ cabs*	*Buses*	*Goods carriages*	*Tractors/ others*	*Total*
Ludhiana district							
01.04.1985	81169	2147	8158	478	4491	23152	119585
01.04.1990	200783	4518	19237	618	8289	32065	265510
01.04.1995	297683	6594	29013	806	11903	38174	384173
01.04.2002	527444	13824	79327	1367	18216	45780	685958
Nagpur district							
31.03.1985	69916	2482	9523	657	8435	1090	92103
31.03.1990	164325	5994	14834	843	12178	1991	200165
31.03.1995	254468	8997	21169	1593	14962	2839	304038
31.03.2002	464831	15293	42626	3235	23057	5066	554108
Nasik district							
31.3.1985	35882	3212	10042	706	11430	4322	65594
31.3.1990	87333	7484	14758	1098	15763	7290	133726
31.3.1995	139336	11033	18833	1045	20283	11570	202100
31.3.2002	270198	22981	41781	1281	33105	23833	393179
Patna district							
01.04.1985	32449	11680	6110	1236	5677	1090	58243
01.04.1990	54081	17622	12213	2460	11907	1740	100023
01.04.1995	91588	23684	22964	6918	22022	3523	170698
01.04.2002	195894	28776	46394	8089	26010	8381	313544
Pune district							
31.3.1985	144398	13815	25065	2625	24505	2033	212441
31.3.1990	327281	24613	41248	3728	32245	5022	434137
31.3.1995	474715	39427	64651	7689	38119	8968	633479
31.3.2002	851746	71238	132089	10000	58550	18211	1140034
Surat district							
01.04.1985	78445	6349	8980	124	11976	5267	111141
01.04.1990	200238	12706	18833	182	18232	7499	257690
01.04.1995	350763	19160	33463	274	27216	10750	441626
01.04.2002	696418	38275	76456	1399	41529	14949	869026

Urban agglomeration district	*Two-wheelers*	*Autos/ tempos*	*Cars/ cabs*	*Buses*	*Goods carriages*	*Tractors/ others*	*Total*
Vadodara district							
01.04.1985	84713	9159	10358	369	10032	13630	128261
01.04.1990	167012	14805	20886	644	15160	16985	235492
01.04.1995	263390	17784	32582	986	22174	20182	357098
01.04.2001	455501	22052	59623	1478	36144	31177	605975
Varanasi district							
01.04.1985	47220	3000	2940	304	1274	2945	57683
01.04.1990	78700	4526	5876	605	2672	4703	97082
01.04.1995	133280	6083	11049	1701	4942	9502	166575
01.04.2002	285068	7391	22322	1989	5837	22648	345255
Viskhapatnam district							
01.04.1985	93964	2810	7060	501	3430	1086	108851
01.04.1990	1269423906		9424	733	4630	1226	146861
01.04.1995	148885	4650	12184	839	5107	1462	173127
01.04.2002	298693	12851	27525	1123	10474	4002	354668

Source : Petroleum Planning and Analysis Cell (PPAC), MoP&NG.

It can be seen that vehicle population and vehicle mix vary substantially. In cities like Mumbai and Kolkata, the numbers of two wheelers as percentage to total registered vehicles is substantially low but is relatively smaller in cities like Pune, Kanpur and Surat. The city transport vehicles like auto/tempo, city taxi/maxi cabs, city buses are in large numbers in cities like Delhi, Kolkata, Bangalore, Chennai, Ahmedabad and Hyderabad compared to medium sized cities.

The mega cities and many other cities suffer from unacceptable levels of pollution on a number of days every year. According to CPCB, the cities of Surat & Delhi, Howrah have critical levels of SO_2 is NO_2 and SPM high almost in all major cities of Gujarat, Himachal Pradesh, Madhya Pradesh, Rajasthan, West Bengal and Delhi.

Small And Deadly: Over half the ultrafine particles are emitted by diesel vehicles.

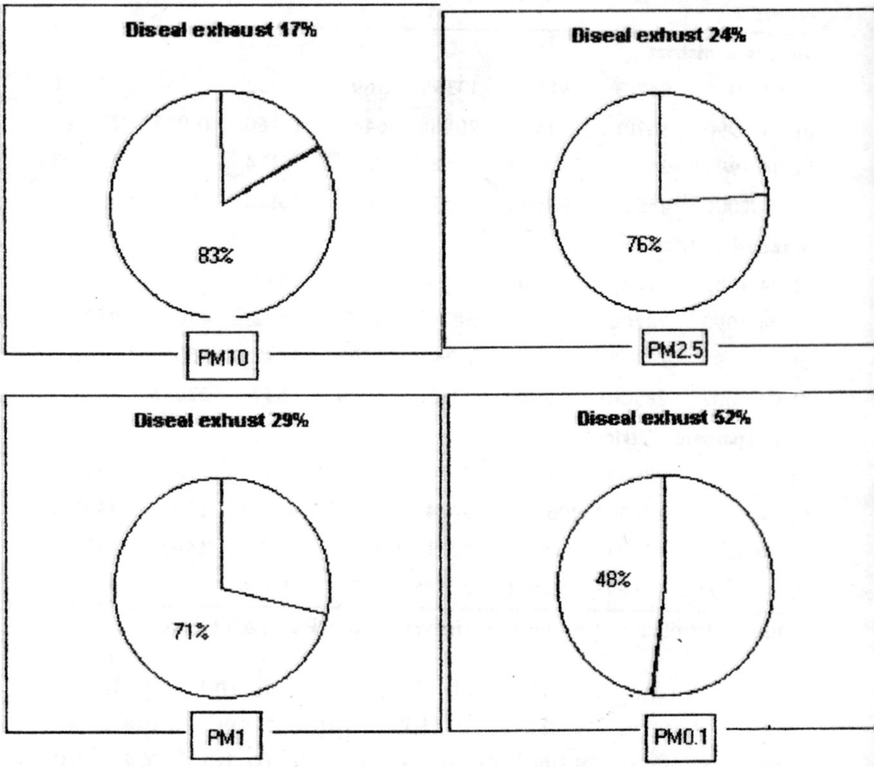

Fig. 8 : Dieal exhaust. Source : Michael Walsh, 2000

The biggest threat to public health is actually from the vehicular emission. The fine particles that cannot be seen are cutting our lives shorter. A study by Harvard School of Public Health and other instituations found that fine particles from vehicles have strongest effect on daily mortality. A mere increase of 10 micrograms per cubic m.i.e. PM10, PM2.5, adding to lung cancer by 8%, heart disease by 6% and all deaths by 4% was published in Journal of American Medical Association. (The study was based on data collected by American Cancer Society, it was 16 years about 500,000 people and 116 metropolitan area).

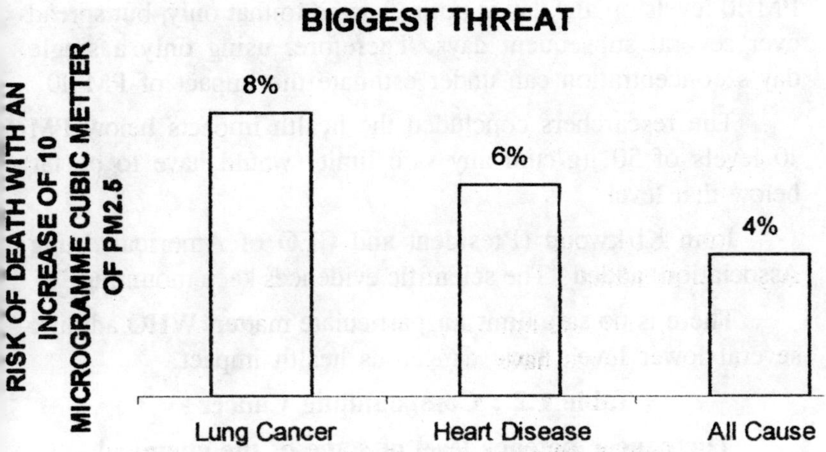

Fig. 9 : Biggest Threat.

Source : C.A. Pope et al. 2002, JAMA, Vol. 287, No.9

The US-based Health Institute funded a study to find out the effects of PM10 alone and in combination with gaseous air pollutants in over 20 small and 90 large cities. The study was published in 2000.

Both the 20 cities and 90 cities analyses showed similar resutls: an average 0.5 per cent increase in overall mortality for every 10 micrograms per cubic meter (µg/cum) increase in PM 10 measured the day before death. This effect was slightly greater for deaths due to heart and lung diseases than for total deaths. The researches found that these tiny particles were wreaking havoc on human health quite independently of other air pollution.

They also studied the effects of PM 10 on hospitalization of those above 65 years in 14 cities. There was about one per cent increase in admission for cardiovascular diseases and about two per cent for pneumonia and chronic obstructive pulmonary diseases for each 10 µg/m increase PM 10. Curiosuly, the study found by per cent or more at concentration less than 50 µg/cum.

The analyses also showed that the effect of an increase in PM 10 levels on any day is not restricted to that only, but spread over several subsequent days. Therefore, using only a single day's concentration can under estimate the impact of PM 10.

The researchers concluded the health impacts below PM 10 levels of 50 μg/cum any safe limit would have to be far below that level.

John Kirkwood (President and CEO of American Lung Association) added "The scientific evidences keep mounting."

There is no safe limit for particulate matter. WHO admits, several lower levels have dangerous health impact.

Table 1.2 : Compounding Cancer

The cancer potency level of some of the chemical compounds found in diesel and petrol emission as designed by various environmental institutes

Compound	*US EPA 1990*	*US EPA 1999*	*CARB*	*CAPOCA*	*Sweden*
Benzene	1	1	1	1	1
1,3-burtadiene	34	36	6	10	20
Formaldehyde	1.6	1.67	0.2	0.45	6
Acetaldehyde	0.27	0.28	0.1	0.1	0.25
Ethene	-	0.28	0.1	0.1	025
Propane	-	0.64	-	0.5	4.5
Propane	-	0.64	-	0.5	4.5

Note :

The cancer potency of each compound has been calculated in relation to the cancer potency of benzene, a known carcinogen

Califonia Air Pollution Control Officers Association; Sweden: University of Stockholm

Source : Peter Ahlvik and Ake Branding 1999, Cancer Risk Index for Passanger Car in India, Ecotraffic R&D AB, Stockholm, Sweden

Table 1.3 : The Cancer index....

The relative cancer potency of particulate matter from diesel exhaust is higher than the total carcinogenic emission from petrol vehicles

Source	*Parti-culates*	*Ben-zene*	*Alkenes*	*Alde-hydes*	*PAC*	*Total*
Gasoline (SI)	5.1	2.0	61	3.7	28	100
Ethanol(SI)	2.3	0.8	22	10.3	19	55
Methanol (SI)	1.9	0.4	3	22.0	19	46
Methane (SI)	1.5	0.1	2	3.0	13	19
Diesel(CI)	121.5	0.4	23	18.4	72	235

Note : PAC Polycyclic aromatic hydrocarbons

Source : Peter Ahvik and Ake Branding 1999, Cancer Risk Index Cars in India, Ecotraffic R&D AB, Stockholm, Sweden

1.4 Why SO_2 is dangerous

A study by USEPA shows that fine particles contains more of sulphates and nitrates-classified by is WHO having serious health impatcs. More of these and other combustion-related chemicals make fine particles more dangerous than PM 10.

The toxic story/ the nightmare goes like this - the fine particles have more surface area then relatively large parti-cles, which makes it more ideal substrate for toxic chemicals which deposit and stick on to surface of the particles. Many known to be carciongenic like Poly cyclic Aromatic Hydrocar-ous (PAHs). There are found more near to diesel vehicles whose ultra fine particles carry toxic to respiratory system (Columbia School of Public Health, New York University, Medical centre and some health research institutes.)

Fig. 10 : Composition of :

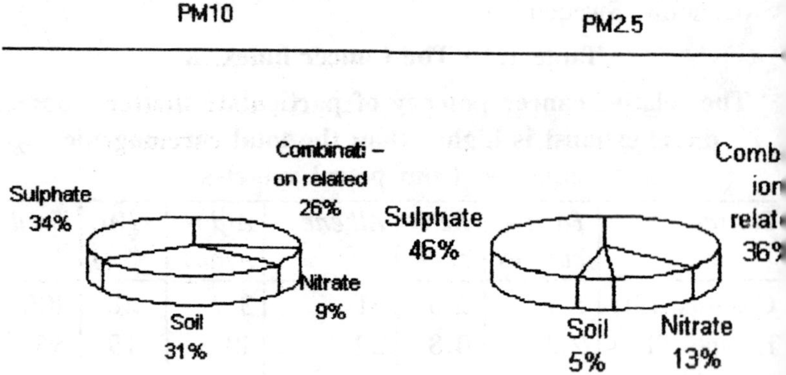

Source : Anon 1997, USEPA

Diesel is considered to be carcinogenic declared by several international organization to name a few are The National Toxicology Programme, The California Environment Protection Agency, California Air Recourses Board, U.S. Environmental Protection Agency etc.

In our country CPCB monitors air quality and PM_{10} data only from 1999 for first time for the whole country. However, data are available in for limited cities. Thus, out of 14 cities data available, 13 cities have recorded critical level of PM_{10}.

The magnitude of consequent health impacts can be horrifying as discussed earlier, Diesel, being major source of fine particulates. In our country diesel consumption is higher (about 6 times more than petrol). Though there are a few studies available, which points towards malady of gigantic proportions.

* One person dies every hour in Delhi due to air choked with particles.
* 25,000 people die ever year in 36 Indian cities due to high level of SPM.

Fig. 11 : Path of a Particle.

How particles trigger health effects one they reach the lungs is not yet clear. There are a number of hypotheses though. A new study published in Circulation 9th January 2002) has found that ultrafine particles may pass into blood circulation and thus exert direct effects on the heart and vessels

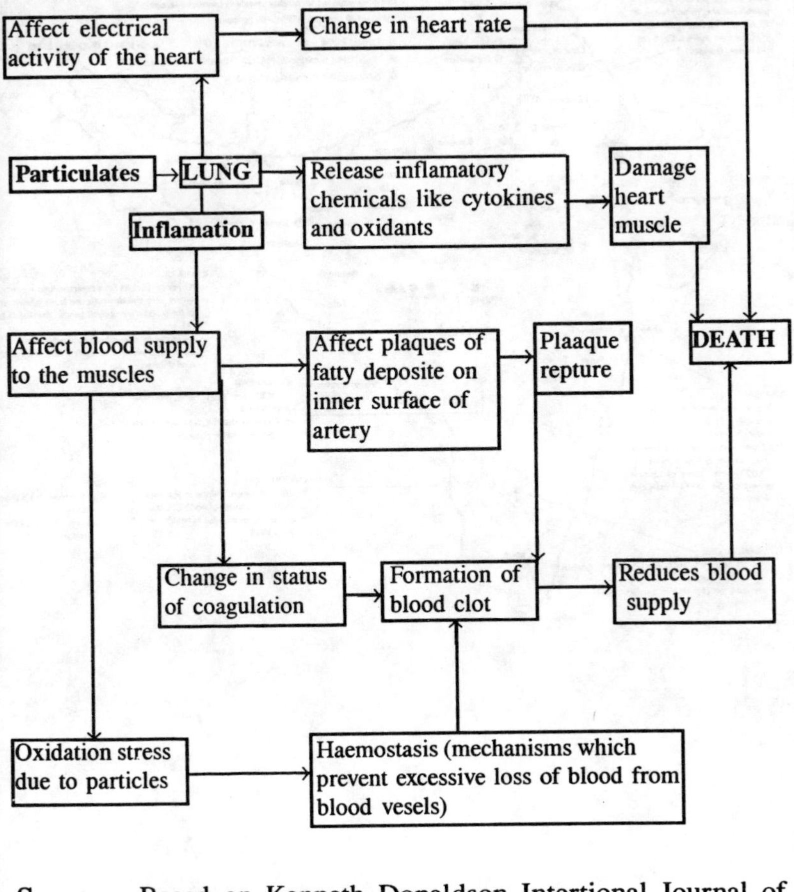

Source : Based on Kenneth Donaldson Intertional Journal of Hygiene & Environmental Health Vol. 203

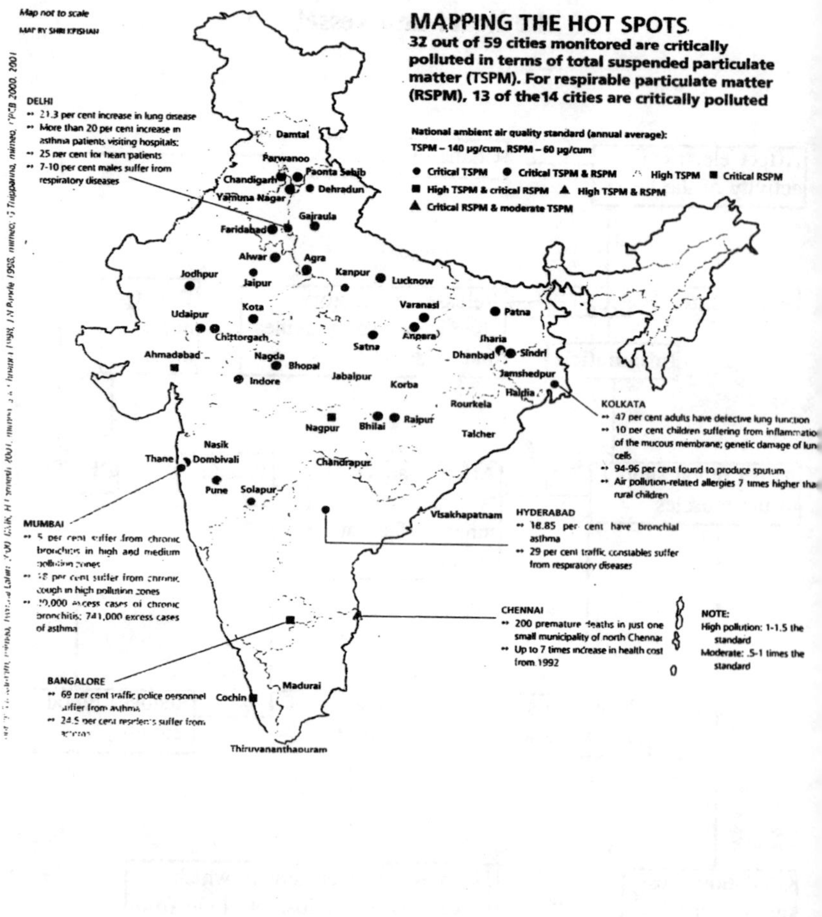

Fig. 12 : Mapping of the Hot Spots.

* Over all respiratory problem increased in Banglore from 9% in 1979 to 24.5% in 1994.
* MoEF have related following facts Epidemiological study conducted. MoEF has initiated the environmental epidemiological studies in 7 critically polluted area viz. Vapi (Gujarat), Angul-Talcher (Orissa), Chembur (Mumbai), Coachin (Kerla), Kanpur(UP), Mandi-Gowindgarh (Punjab), Najafgarh drain basin Delhi and also in Pune. The initial feedback from the studies indicate that the incidence of symptomatic morbidity (eye irriation, respiratory problem, and skin/irritation) is higher in areas of industrial activity. However, no conclusinve data on morbidity and mortality rates could be established having direct correlation with the environmental pollution (MoEF 2000b).

The studies conducted about such correltaion often remain controversial uncertainly persists whether air pollution causes health problem.

It is a reason enough to operate on precautionary principle and reduce levels of air pollution and exposure to them.

Prof. V. Ramlingaswami. (Former director of AIIMS, President of National Institute of Immunology as well as Former Director of ICMR) released document expressing concern over harmful effect of Air pollution in Delhi, Pointing out "There is urgent need for comprehensive epidemiological studies to show how ambient air pollution is affecting peoples health and to quantitate this information and provide policy tools for air quality planning."

Supreme Court ruling of April 5,2002, is momentous. The rulling hits hard to government incompetence even to perform its administrative role reminding it of its fundamental duty to protect right to life and thus people health. This notable ruling that upholds the supremacy of human health must not be diluted only to protect economic interest.

The right to clean and healthy environment is a part of right to life enshined in the Indian constitution.

1.6 Conclusion :

In country like ours, where resources are scare relatively to variety of developmental objectives, it is of special importance to carefully set air pollution control policies and priorities according to health impacts and anticipated benefits.

* Vehicular pollution control deserves top priority.
* Pollution load from vehicular emission can be known to a fair degree of accuracy there is hardly reliable data even for major cities on air pollution.
* A Comprehensive urban air quality mangement strategy should be formulated using Urban planning, ambient air quality, emission norms.
* The engines used traffic mangement system poor road conditions, outdated technologies also add to air pollution.
* The system of checking tail pipes in itself is flamed providing for greater scope for corruption, based on weak exhaust nomes.
* Cleaner energy policies needs to be introduced.

1.7 Suggestions :

The path to change for better Environmental plans and regulations are essential to provide a conducive frame work or benchmark for change but they are of little use unless they are implemented/enforced. The Pollution Board, Municipalities are weak to discharge their responsibilites. They need to be made more stronger by transparency, public hearings, citizens participation budgetary support and autonomy.

1. Strengthening of monitoring network

The monitoring network requires a massive quality control programme and expansion of its operations to cover new stations as well as more pollutants (e.g., $RPM_{2.5}$, O_3, Pb, CO and hydrocarbons such as benzene and PAHs) on a regular basis. Smaller cities should also be covered so that preventive measures could be taken before the pollution problem becomes acute.

2. Information dissemination/mass awareness/training

State-of-the-art technology should be used for wider dissemination of environmental information. Transparency and access to the data to be improved. Measures such as pollution bulletins and air pollution forecast should be started on a regular basis.

Massive thrust should be provided to mass awareness campaigns involving community organization such as residents associations, students, voluntary bodies and NGOs. Strategies and action plans for implemention should be devised.

Support measures such as training and education for the industry, govermental agencies, and the public, as well as greater coordination among institutions, are important.

3. Stringent emission norms for new vehicles are needed

Thus, it is imperative that both fuel specification and engine technologies go head to head.

4. Inspection and Maintenance is important step towards emission control.

It needs therefore to establishe effective and adequate periodic inspection and Maintenance programme.

5. Epidemiological studies should be undertaken to develop dose

Response relationship which will help to develop in appropriate air quality standards.

REFRENCES

1. Anon 1997; United States Environment Protection Agency, USA.
2. Ghose C. (2002): Down to Earth, April 15, 2002, CSE, Delhi.
3. Kenneth D. *et al.* (2001): International Journal of Hygiene and Environmental Health : 203, USA.

4. Peter A. & Ake B. (1999): Cancer Risk Index for Passenger Cars in India, Ecotraffic R&D AB, Stockholm, Sweden.
5. Samet J. et al (2002): Health effects Insitute Research Report No. 94, USA.
6. Mukherjee U. Lokhande S.L. A. Ganvelu, M.M. Alam and S.S. Bala (2002): Air Quality Trend at Vadodara City in Gujarat (CPCB).
7. *http://www.1hh. org*

16

An Efficient Method to Detect Pollution Load of Bio-particles in Indoor Air

Arun Arya and Timir R. Shah

Microbes constitute an integral part of biotic component of our ecosystem. These are found in soil, water and air. These minuscular life forms naturally find their way in most places of man's work and leisure and interact with him in various ways. Monitoring the quality of ambient air for the presence of microorganisms is thus necessary so that seri-ous health hazards could be avoided in hospitals. The infor-mation will be of great use in heavily populated areas like picture theatres, museums, libraries and in some industries as well as sterile areas like operation theatres and tissue culture laboratories etc.

An experiment was conducted in Egypto babilonian and picture galleries of Baroda Museum on 10th March 2003. Hi Air sampler system mark II was used and comparison was made with petridish exposure method. This simple instrument is marketed by Hi Media Laboratories Ltd., Mumbai. It operates on the prin-ciple of impaction. In petri dishes growth of viable microorganisms is recorded due to settling of microoganisms by gravity fall. Bacterial and fungal count was calculated by using strips with SCA and SAB media respectively. Agar medium strip is inserted peripherally into the slot so that agar surface faces the impeller. It sucks 280 liters of air per minute. Total bacterial count was $18/ft^3$ near the mummy chamber as compared to $28/ft^3$ at far end. In picture gallery the count was $25/ft^3$.The fungal colonies were less $4/ft^3$ in mummy gallery and $9/ft^3$ in picture gallery. This method offers a better alternative for quantitative analysis of microbes than the conventional petridish exposure method. The instrument is easy to handle. The visual readings may be taken twice (at an interval of 24h) from same strip and data should be statistically analyzed to give better results.

Introduction

The Baroda Museum and Picture Gallery is famous for its collection of Europian oil paintings all over Asia. The buildings of Museum are situated in pastoral environment of Sayajipark. This Museum was built by Sir Sayajirao Gaekwad III in Indo-Saracenic style of architecture. Baroda Museum is one of the seven museums in the country where Egyptian Mummies are kept for display.

Indoor aeromycoflora has attracted the attention of aerobiologists like Arya *et al.* (1988), Bhuvaneswari and Vittal (2001), Chanda (1992), Gregory (1973), Knox (1979), Meshram *et al.* (2001), Saoji and Sawane, (2001), Shah *et al.* (1996), Spiksma (1980), and Subbaraman, (1990) have emphasized the importance of monitoring such biopollutants in different environments. These biopollutants not only cause environ-mental pollution but also can be disseminated by the action of wind. Biodeterioration of cultural property may result by these notorious fungal organisms. At the threshold of new millenium we are concerned to conserve these most valuable links of human civilization. Since these rare exam-ples will only help to educate the generations yet to come about human life in the ancient past. We should be aware that any biodeteriorated object may act as a small or large bio-industry emitting not only polluted water or gases but living microoganisms with a potential to produce another such unit within a short period.

The results of experiment conducted by Hi Air sampler in Egypto-babylonian and picture galleries of Baroda Museum and picture gallery on 10th March 2003 are shown in the table 1 and histogram 1. Hi Air sampler system make II was used and com-parison was made with petridish exposure method. Usually we do not increase the time peiod of petri dish exposure method as we may get large number of mixed colonies which are difficult to count.

Materials and Methods

Hi Air sampler: The Hi Air Sampler operates on the principle of impaction. The air under examination is sucked by the impeller (Plate 1 Photo 1. and 2) in tornado-like spiralling conical form and the particles contained in it are centrifugally impacted against inward facing peripheral agar medium strip. The impellar speed of 4100 rpm is so adjusted that 28 litre of air is sampled every minute. The sampling volume corresponds to 40 litre/min of the seperation vol i.e. 1/7th of the sampling volume-based on the mathematical computation in the design principle.

Sampling was done at two different places in Egypto-babilonian and 4 places in picture gallery. Air sampling was also done by Gravity fall method by exposing petridishes for 10 min. The CFUs (Colony Forming Units) could be visually counted by placing the strip (Plate III) on a light table/colony counter. The organisms detected/unit vol of air can then be calculated as under:

$$\text{CFU/litre} = \frac{\text{Colonies on agar strip}}{\text{40X Sampling time (min)}}$$

(1 minute correspond to 40 litre of air separtion volume)

$$\text{CFU/ft}^3 = \frac{\text{Colonies on agar strip X 0.708}}{\text{Sampling time in minutes}}$$

$$\text{CFU / m}^3 = \frac{\text{Colonies on agar strip X 25}}{\text{Sampling time in minutes}}$$

Besides PDA medium following two media were used in the study :

1. Soybean casein digest agar medium
   (Tryptone Soy agar for bacteria)

Casein enzymic hydrolysate	15g
Peptic digest of soy bean meal	05g
NaCl	05g
Agar	15g
Ditilled water	1000ml
pH	07

2. Sabourd's Chloramphenical agar medum (For Yeasts and Moulds)

Casein enzymic hydrolysate	05g
Peptic digest of animal tissue	05g
Dextrose	40g
Chloramphenicol	0.05g
Agar	15g
Distilled water	1000 ml
pH	5.6

Table 1: Number of colony forming units observed at Egypto-babylonian Gallery and Picture Gallery after 48 h incubation for bacteria and 72h for fungi

SI. No.	*No. of Colonies on SCA*	*CFU/ft^3 (Bacteria)*	*No. of Colonies on SAB*	*CFU/ft^3 (Fungi)*
Samples collected from Egypto-babylonian gallery				
1.	126	17.84	11	02
2.	198	28.04	25	3.5
Samples collected from Picture Gallery				
3.	186	25	24	3.5
4.	173	24.49	32	4.53

(Values represented are average of 5 strips after run of instrument for 5 min.)

Results And Discussion

Rich cultural heritage, comprising of monuments, sculpture, paintings, illustrated manuscripts on paper and palm leaf draws our immediate attention. The task of conservation is indeed challenging (Subbaraman 1993). The causes of deterioration are equally important to be known clearly. very little work is done to identify the load of biopollutant, particularly Number of Fungi or Bacteria per Cu. ft. of air in any Museum room or gallery.

Total colony forming units (CFUs) were detected by Hi Air sampler and fungal count was also taken by petridish exposure method in two galleris of Museum in Baroda. Upper floor houses paintings related to 15-18th Cen and are depicted in this big hall. On right hand side of entrance hall, sampling was done near sculpture of French modern art, The bathing Women by Jean Vezien. The nudity in European art generally indicates a heroic subject, mostly taken from Ancient Greek mythology. Another statue The judgement of Paris, is placed in the hall. It holds an apple the statute of Aphrodite, it has doves at her feet which are sacred animals, or the Vahanas.

Total count for fungi ranged from 4-5, *Rhizopus nigricans* dominated followed by Dematiatious Hyphomycetes genera like *Cladosporium* and *Alternaria,* these belong to group Deuteromycotina. *Aspergillus niger* and *A. flavus* were also present belonging to Ascomycotina. *Aspergillus* spp. deteriorates paper and their presence has been reported from indoor air of Baroda Museum (Arya *et al.* 2001). They found presence of *E. niveia* (sexual stage of *Aspergillus*) with deteriorating Egyptian mummy in 1999. The different paintings use glue & starch and these are used in other museum objects, which may be utilized as raw material by the fungi. These fungal organisms can grow in such low moisture content as 7-9% (Nair 1971).

Greathouse and Ames (1945) described fabric deterioration by 13 described, 3 new spp. of *Chaetomium*, a genera belonging to Chaetomiales of Ascomycotina. According to Kowalik (1980) development of fungi on paper depends on pH of the objects. Any fungal attack on museum attack may be due to:

1. Supply of food material or suitable nutrition
2. Suitable temperature
3. Suitable moisture
4. Presence of O_2
5. Presence of some other source of microbes / inoculum

Conclusions

The method is fast and quite reliable as data from petridish exposure method also gave similar results. The instrument is handy and easy to operate by electricity or by battery. The medium used and time required also needs to be further worked out. The time taken into account 72h was not sufficient for growth of many fungi and only growth of fast filamentous zygomycotina member like *Rhizopus* was seen growing. The instrument is ideal for checking pollution load quantitatively in certain other sensitive areas like Hospitals and Library in different cities. Its use is recommended to know the biotic load of pollutants in indoor air.

Acknowledgements

The authors are thankful to Baroda Museum and Picture gallery authorities for giving permission for sampling. Thanks are also due to Director, Choksi laboratories Ltd. and Head, Department of Botany, The Maharaja Sayajirao University of Baroda to provide necessary facilities to undertake this project.

REFERENCES

Arya, A., Bhowmik, S.K. and Shah, A.R. 1988 Biodeterioration of Paintings, Geobios New Reports 7:179-180

Arya, A. Shah, A.R. and Sadasivan, S. 2001 House Dust—A potential source of mould allergens in house environments (Abstr,) Indian J. Aerobiol. 14:44

Chanda, S. 1922. Aerobilogy: an inter and multidisciplinary approach. Indian J. Aerobiol. sp. Vol. 1-10 pp.

Greathouse, G.A. and Ames, L.M. 1945 Fabric deterioration by thirteen described and three new spp. of *Chaetomium.* Mycologia 37: 138-155.

Gregory, P.H. 1973 The Microbiology of the atmosphere, Leonord Hill Books, Aylesbury, England 2nd Ed. pp. 377.

Knox, R.B. 1979 Pollen Allergy, Arnold, London

Kowalik, R. 1980 Microbiodeterioration of Library materials part II Microbiodeterioration of basic organic materials ch. IV Restaurator 4: 135-215.

Meshram, B.M., Meshram, S. and Bagwan 2001 Aeroallergens and incidences of allergic disorders Abstr. Indian J. Aerobiol. 14:43.

Nair, S.M. 1971 In: Biodeterioration of Materials (eds) A.H. Walters & E.H.H. Plas, Applied Science, London, U.K. 2: 401-421

Saoji, A.A.and Sanwane A.M. 2001 Control of post harvest green mold of citrus fruit : a comperative study. Indian J. Aerobiol. 14:16-19

Shah, N.R., Arya A., Shah, A.R. and Bhowmik, S.K. 1996 A study of atmospheric fungal flora and biodeterioration n different museums of Baroda. In: Pers. Biol. Sci. (eds) V. Rai, M.L. Naik and C. Manoharachary, Raipur University. 189-196

Spieksma, F.T.M. 1980 Importance of aerobiological studies for the prediction of human diseases. Aerobiol. Symp. Munich. 307-315.

Subbaraman, S. 1993 Conservation of Mural paintings. Curr. Sci. 64:736-753.

Plate I

Photo 1. Hi Air Sampler seen during use.

Photo 2. Impeller Assembly showing inner wheel.

Plate II

Photo 1. A, impeller; B, instrument showing digital minute display; C, A person showing removal of Agar strip from impeller.

Plate III

Photo 1. Sabourd's medium showing growth of fungi in Egypto-babylonian Gallery

Photo 2. Sabourd's medium showing growth of fungi in picture Gallery of Baroda Museum.

Plate IV

Photo 1. Petri dishes showing growth of *Rhizopus* in oine and in another bacteria and fungi present in Egypto-babylonian Gallery

Photo 2. Part of strip containing SCA medium showing growth of Bacteria in Egyptobabylonian Gallery.

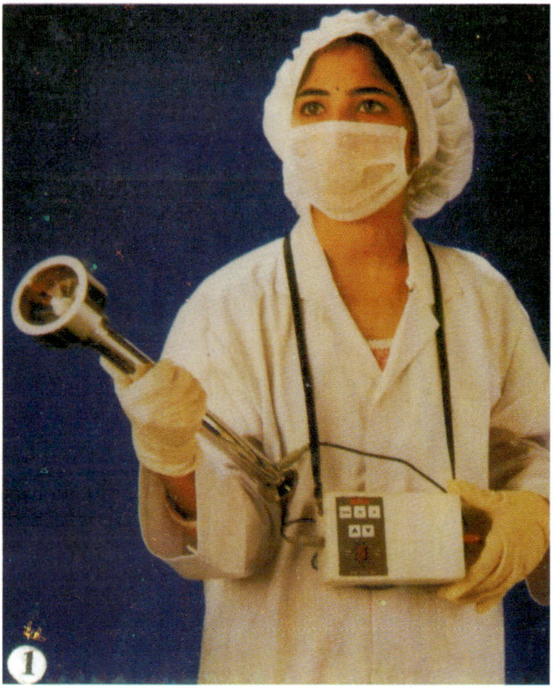

Pl. 1A.Hi Air Sampler seen during use.

B. Impeller Assembly showing inner wheel.

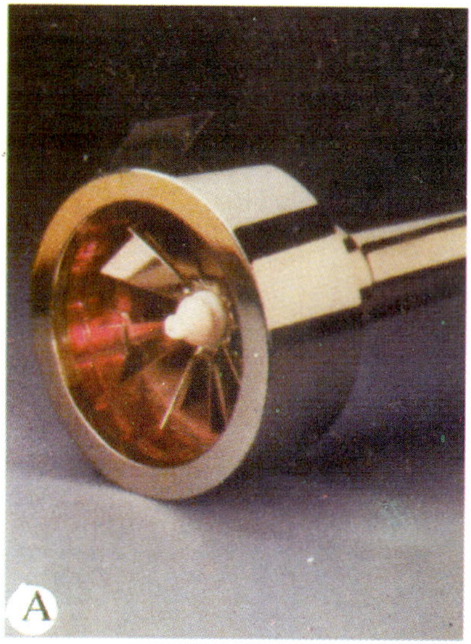

Pl. 2A. Impeller,

B. Instrument showing digital minute display.

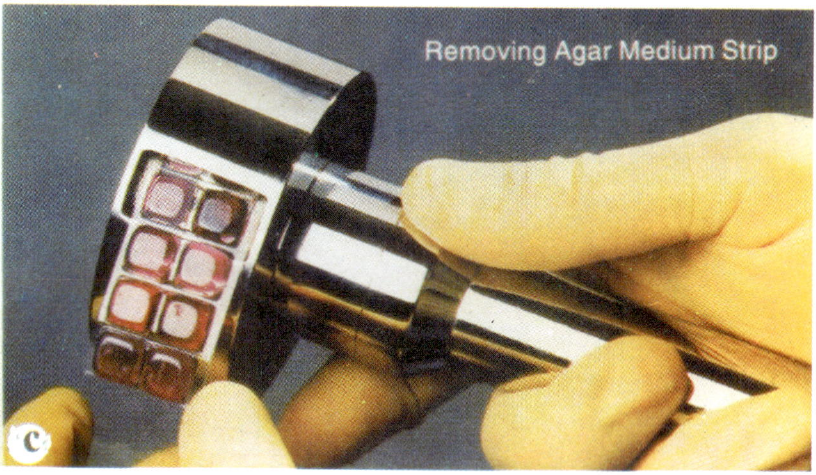

C. A person showing removal of Agar strip from impeller.

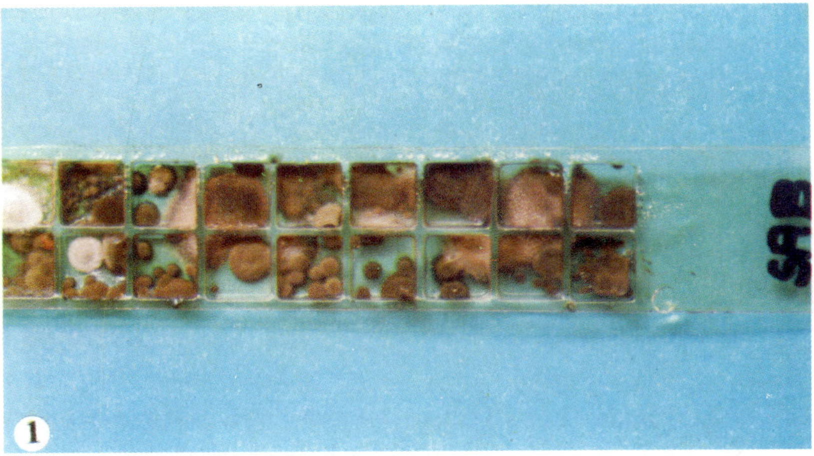

Pl. 3A.Sabourd's medium showing growth of fungi in Egypto-babylonian Gallery

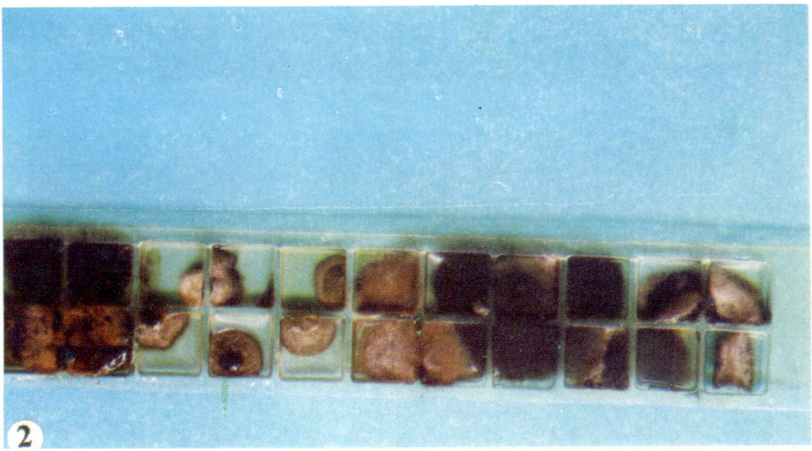

B.. Sabourd's medium showing growth of fungi in picture Gallery of Baroda Museum.

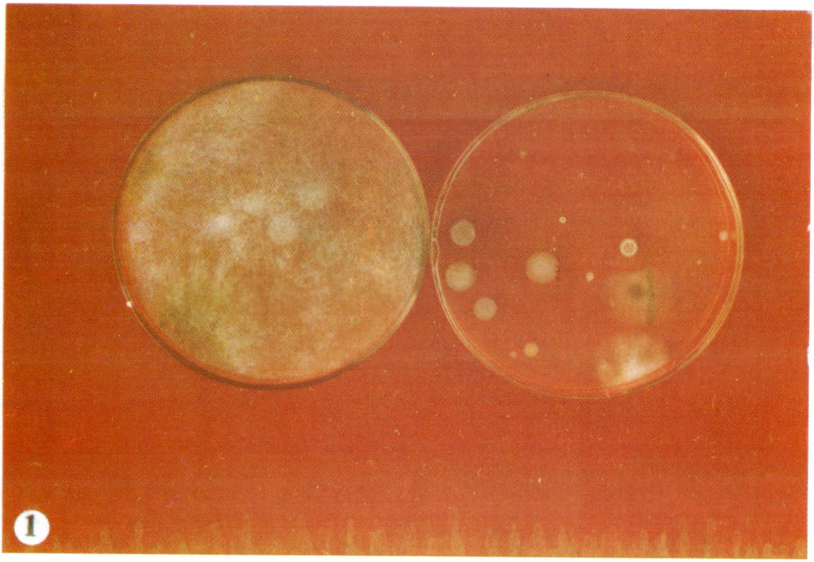

Pl. 4A. Petri dishes showing growth of Rhizopus in one and in another bacteria and fungi are present in Egyptobabylonian Gallery

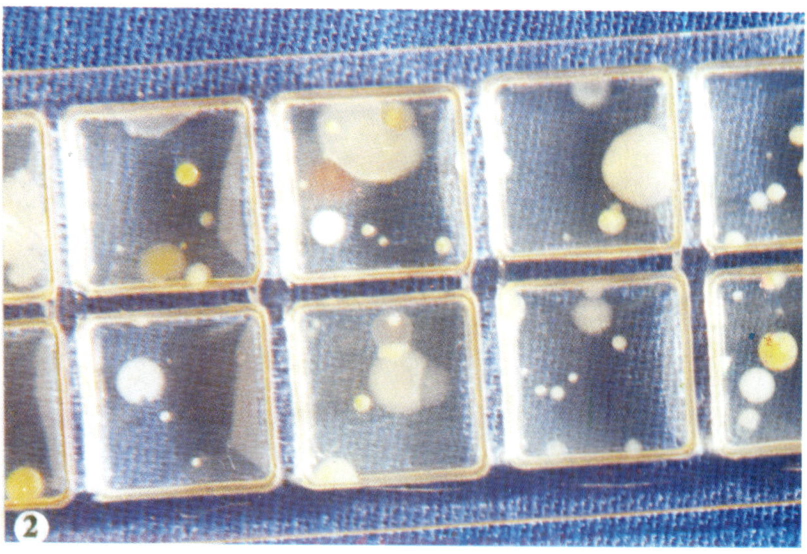

B. Part of strip containing SCA medium showing growth of Bacteria present in Egyptobabylonian Gallery.

17

Biological Filtration of Indoor Air Pollution Agents

M. N. Thaker and Y. T. Jasrai

People of most developed and developing countries spend a major fraction of their life inside buildings, may it be office, home, club, restaurant or any other concrete structure. The census of 1930 in United States of America revealed that 80% of Americans lived on farms, but just within 2 decades i.e. by 1950, the scenario had completely changed and 80% of Americans were in cities leaving just 20% of its total population to breathe clean air. The scenario is no different in India with the recent urbanization and its unprecedented economic growth and participation in the global economy. Though percentage wise still a major population of the country inhabits rural areas but with a population of 100 crores the number of individuals in cities far exceeds those in USA. Implicit in this urbanization is a large and rapid shift from working in fields under the open sky to working indoors in a closed environment -the segregation of humans from the natural environment into artificial, machine operated, fossil fuel run environments. The development of such segregating shells is beyond any compari-sons in the history of life on earth. Today, people living in industrialized countries spend over 90% of their lives inside buildings either in office, restaurants, public places or at home, which amounts to over 65 years of an average human life. Of the remaining 10% of the life, a considerable part in most cases is spend traveling on vehicles, polluting the external environ-ment and breathing the same, simply to add to the problems (Ulrich *et al.* 1991). So while debating on air pollution and air quality and our health, indoor air pollution becomes an issue of major concern. This is not to say outdoor air quality is not important, but coupled with indoor air quality make life miserable.

INTRODUCTION:

Indoor air pollution is not a very old area of research for the environmentalists. Till early 80's there is hardly any apprehension expressed or report of research conducted on this aspect, which reflects the ignorance about the matter in the scientific community of this major concern of today.

The present position of India with a very rapid growth and industrialization is no different with that of USA in mid 20th century. The rapid industrialization accompanied increased migration of rural people towards cities in western countries. In order to accommodate and satisfy the need of space for such large human population in limited land area the cities started growing more in height (vertical) than in its width (horizontal) or in other words their volume increased more than the area. The concept of skyscrapers started becoming very popular. They were readily accepted by masses since they could provide a larger area of access at a cheaper rate using a limited land area. Further, the energy crises of 70's in the west led to construction of super insulated buildings so as to lower down on the energy consum-ption required for maintaining ambient internal temperatures against extreme external environment. These insulated high raised buildings proved to be very successful in satisfying the need of that time and easily achieved global acceptance of most corporate and construction companies of developing and developed nations and the trend has not changed yet.

But these changes lead to curtailment of readily available natural resources for the people occupying those buildings.

The sunlight and fresh air were replaced by the electric bulbs and recycled air of the filters respectively.

Indoor Pollutants-sources and consequences : The interiors of any office or a home has several sources of pollution that an individual might not be aware of. Majority of them emit volatile organic compounds and so such hazardous compounds have become ubiquitous indoors. The most common pollutants that have been found and studied as an indoor pollutants are Trichloroethylene, Benzene and Formaldehyde. Major sources of each of these hazardous chemicals and the threats caused to human health due to their presence in the indoor atmosphere are as follows:

Table-1 : Indoor air concentrations of chemicals (in µg/l) found in various buildings

Chemicals	*Hospitals*	*Nursing Homes*	*Office Buildings*
Chloroform	---	0.004	0.002
Trichloroethylene	0.002	0.001	0.005
Benzene	0.003	0.003	0.005
Xylene	0.013	0.005	0.022
Formaldehyde	0.106	0.081	0.173

1. Trichloroethylene (TCE)—It is a commercial product found in a wide variety of industrial uses. Over 90 percent of the TCE produced is used in the metal decreasing and dry cleaning industries. In addition, it is used in **printing inks, paints, lacquers, varnishes**, and **adhesives**. In 1975 the National Cancer Institute, USA reported that an unusually high incidence of hepatocellular carcinoma was observed in mice given TCE by gastric intubation and now considers this chemical as a potent liver carcinogen.

2. Benzene—It is a very commonly used solvent and is also present in many common items including **gasoline**, **inks**, **oils**, **paints**, **plastics**, and **rubber**. In addition it is used in the manufacture of detergents, explosives, pharmaceuticals, and dyes.

Benzene has long been known to irritate the skin and eyes.

In addition, it has been shown to be mutagenic to bacterial cell culture and has shown embryotoxic activity and carcinogenicity. Evidence also exists that benzene may be a contributing factor in chromosomal aberrations and leukemia in human. Repeated skin contact with benzene will cause drying, inflammation, blistering and dermatitis. Acute inhalation of high levels of benzene has been reported to cause dizziness, weakness, euphoria, headache, nausea, blurred vision, respiratory diseases, tremors, irregular heartbeat, liver and kidney damage, paralysis and unconsciousness. In animal tests, inhalation of benzene led to cataract formation and diseases of the blood and lymphatic systems. Chronic exposure to even relatively low levels causes headaches, loss of appetite, drowsiness, nervousness, psychological disturbances and diseases of the blood system, including anemia and bone marrow diseases.

3. Formaldehyde - It is a ubiquitous chemical found in virtually all indoor environments. The major sources that have been reported and publicized include urea-formaldehyde foam insulation (UFFI) and particle board or pressed wood products used today in manufacturing of the office furniture. It is used in consumer paper products that have been treated with UF resins, including grocery bags, waxed papers, facial tissues and paper towels. Many common household cleaning agents contain formaldehyde. UF resins are used as stiffeners, wrinkle resisters, water repellents, fire retardants and adhesive binders in floor coverings, carpet backings and permanent-press clothes. Other sources of formaldehyde include heating and cooking fuels like natural gas, kerosene, and cigarette smoke.

Formaldehyde irritates the mucous membranes of the eyes, nose and throat. It is also a highly reactive chemical which combines with protein and can cause allergic contact dermatitis. The most widely reported symptoms from exposure to high levels of this chemical include irritation of the eyes and headache. Until recently, the most serious of the diseases attributed to formaldehyde exposure was asthma. However, the Environmental Protection Agency (EPA) has recently conducted research that has caused formaldehyde to be strongly suspected of causing a type of throat cancer in long-term occupants of mobile homes.

Toluene and Xylene: They are a part of stationary products, adhesives, floor coverings, computer screens and other instruments. Photocopiers form a major source of toluene and xylene emission.

Toluene and xylene causes frequent headaches and trouble in concentrating as a short term hazard but can affect the nervous system over a longer exposure to these chemicals. (Wolverton *et al.* 1993)

SICK BUILDING SYNDROME:

Besides these pollutants the major problem of concern that had been overlooked by most offices is called as 'sick building syndrome'. It is a sort of occupational problem, wherein people working in buildings with very little or no ventilation and inhaling recycled air exhibit symptoms of typical allergic reactions like itchy eyes, rashes, drowsiness, sinus and respiratory congestion, and headaches (Field *et al.* 1998). Most people working in metro cities of developing and developed countries at some or the other time face this problem, especially if they smoke, but fail to identify it due to ignorance about it.

The Plants for Clean Air Council (PCAC) adds that low indoor humidity is another significant health problem. Dry, winterized air, the group says, irritates nasal membranes, triggers asthma and congestion, and makes people more susceptible to viruses and allergens.

HOT ISLAND SYNDROME:

Concrete jungle of many skyscrapers in a small limited area leaves no scope for dissipation of sun energy picked up throughout the day. The problem is more acute in tropical - subtropical conditions. During night this accumulated heat is released by concrete material of the buildings out at a very low release basis. Thus making such cities to be hot island making conditions not conducive even during night times.

REMEDIES:

1. ARCHITECTURE: One of the good ways to take care of the indoor pollution is a good architecture of the buildings.

May it be office or house or any other public place, care needs to be taken for adequate and appropriate ventilation of the buildings. The design of the construction should also be such that it can take maximum benefits from the naturally available resources. The building material used should be eco-friendly and supporting the concept of clean indoor environment.

Though these changes are possible, but for more than one reason their practical applicability and acceptability is certainly to a very limited extent. Firstly, this concept can be applied to only the buildings under construction or to be constructed in future. But the problem still persists for the huge skyscrapers that are already standing high. For the futuristic buildings, the materials to be used for construction of such high raise buildings needs to be not only light in weight but also durable. Also, it should be cheap; since the whole concept of building BIG revolves around gaining more out of less. It is not possible to sacrifice any of these basic aspects required in construction of high towers, which forms limitation with the eco-friendly materials.

With respect to the design, the good ventilation can very easily bring a permanent solution to the problem without any added inputs.

2. PLANTS:

There has been a great deal of studies done on the potential role of plants in combating the outdoor pollution. The road side plantations, development of parks and gardens, green restora-tion of wastelands are few examples of environmental awareness developed in the local governing authorities and the co-operation of various NGO's in mitigating air pollution (Fig.1) Besides, the strict norms and legislation for the control of industrial pollution with special emphasis on development of greenbelts around the polluting units has made the vital role of plants evident as air purifiers. Most of the plants that have been studied for their resistance against the polluted environment and role in quenching the pollutants include beautiful trees like *Cassias* that form the green belts or *Polyalthia* that form giant screens and the ornamental shrubs like *Bougainvilleas* used for plantation in dividers on highways. The key factor in use of plants is their exclusive ability of performing photosynthesis whereby they convert carbon dioxide a green house gas into sugars and oxygen an important lifeline for all living organisms. They also have a fantastic capability to act as screens for fine particles as they retain them on its surface (Wolverton, 1997). The effective contribution of plants in controlling air pollution has been very well proved from cellular to community level studies.

But while developing strategy for combating indoor air pollution the criteria of plants to be selected needs to be redefined. Plants recommended for cleaning the outdoor environment cannot be selected for the indoors simply due to their huge size and lack of aesthetic value. An ideal plant to be selected, as a biological filter to combat indoor air should possess following features:

1. They should be efficient biological filters that can absorb a spectrum of air pollutants.
2. They should be leafy; there by have larger surface area for absorption.
3. Once absorbed the chemicals should get degraded into non-hazardous forms either by its internal mechanism or through its association with soil microbes.
4. They should not be huge in size since they have to be accommodated in a limited space.
5. They should be slow growing and should inevitably have aesthetic value.

A landmark research on the role of a few selected indoor plants against indoor air pollution was conducted by NASA of USA and supported by Associated Landscape Contractors of America (ALCA). Major emphasis was to use the biological processes as a means for solving the environmental problems in a closed system, to be particular in space habitats. (Wolverton *et al.* 1989)

In a series of preliminary experiments, various indoor ornamental plants were exposed to high levels of toxic gases-Formaldehyde, Benzene and Trichloroethylene, the most common indoor pollutants in urban buildings, discussed earlier. The potted plants were placed in sealed Plexiglas chambers maintaining adequate light and temperature conditions. Known amount of toxic gases were externally supplied in the chamber atmosphere at regular intervals. Not only that the plants were able to withstand the toxic gases, but also the degradation products were recovered from the pot soil analysis at the end of the experiment Wolverton, (1986). Though several plants could exhibit only theoretical results but for some, there was no doubt for their practical acceptability for a particular pollutant.

Table-2: Removal of formaldehyde from sealed chambers by plants grown in potting soil

Common name	*Scientific name*	*Removal Rate** (*μg/hr*)
Areca palm	*Chrysaudocarpus lutescens*	938
Bamboo palm	*Chamaedorea* seifrizii	1350
Corn plant	*Dracaena fragrans* "Massangeana"	938
Dwarf date palm	*Phoenix roebelenii*	1385
English ivy	*Hedera helix*	1120
Janet Craig	*Dracaena deremensis* "Janet Craig"	1328
Lady palm	*Rhapis excelsa*	876
Peace lily	*Spathiphyllum* "Clevelandii"	939
Weeping fig	*Ficus benjamina*	940

Also, the composite role of the 'Potted Plant System' in removal of harmful gases has been suggested. It not only removes the toxin from air but also degrades it. The aerial plant components namely leaves and stem absorb the toxic gases but can supply it to the soil through their roots (Wolverton, 1984). The soil plays a role of storage compartment wherein the toxins are degraded mainly by the microbial activity and by the root exudates.

Plants not only provide an easier, cheaper and sustainable

solution to the problem of indoor air pollution but also are not much demanding in maintenance. This remedy of combating pollution from indoor air can be applied on the buildings to be constructed as well as the ones that already exist.

INDOOR PLANTS:

The Environmental Protection Agency cites indoor air pollution as one of the top five public health threats in America, and the main culprit in the 60 percent rise in asthma over the last decade. The role of plants is not limited to absorbing pollutants, but also plants increase the humidity of their immediate surroundings. Low relative humidity levels, generated by heating systems and air conditioning, irritate sensitive membranes in the nose, increasing susceptibility to assaults by airborne chemicals, viruses and allergens. Frequent colds during winter are often caused by low relative humidity.

The role of plants in converting carbon dioxide into oxygen via photosynthesis has long been established thereby rejuvenating fresh oxygen from the same air. For this reason they have also been termed as green lungs of earth.

Indoor plants not only increase the aesthetic value of the interiors but also have been reported to increase the working efficiency (Lohr *et al.* 1996). Patients suffering from the sick building syndrome are many-a-times suggested to cultivate interest in gardening. Presence of plants in the vicinity at work in a closed environment generates a soothing effect and provides a natural environment that helps in relieving from the problems of such syndromes. The plants for indoors can be replaced from time to time and thereby the sceneric freshness of the place can be maintained.

REFERENCES

1. Field, T., et al. Effect of Indoor Foliage Plants on Health and Discomfort Symptoms Among Office Workers," *Indoors + Built Environment,* 1998, 7:204-206.
2. Lohr, V. I., et al. Interior Plants May Improve Worker Productivity and Reduce Stress in a Windowless Environment, *J. Environ. Hort.,* 1996, 14:97-100.

3. Nakamura, R. and E. Fujii. Studies of the Characteristics of the Electroencephalogram When Observing Potted Plants: *Pelargonium hortorum* "Sprinter Red" and *Begonia evansiana,*" *Technical Bulletin* of *the Faculty* of *Horticulture* of *Chiba University, Japan,* 1990, 43: 177-183.

4. Oyabu, T., et al. Purification *Effect* of Interior Plants for Indoor Air Polluting Chemicals and Environmental Preservation, *4th Intl. Conf. on Eng. Design and Automation,* 2000, (Orlando, FI, July 30-Aug 2) pp. 876-881.

5. Ulrich, Roger S., et al. Stress Recovery During Exposure to Natural and Urban Environments, *J.* of *Environ. Psychology,* 1991, 11:201-230.

6. Wolverton, B. C. *Eco-Friendly Houseplants,* Weidenfeld & Nicolson, London, 1996.

7. Wolverton, B. C. and J. D. Wolverton, Plants and Soil Microorganisms Removal of Formaldehyde, Xylene and Ammonia from the Indoor Environment, *Journal* of *the Mississippi Academy* of *Sciences,* 1993, 38(2): 11-15.

8. Wolverton, B. C., A. Johnson and K. Bounds, Interior Landscape Plants for Indoor Air Pollution Abatement, NASA/ALCA Final Report, *Plants for Clean Air Council,* Davidsonville, Maryland, 1989.

9. Wolverton, B. C., R. C. McDonald and E. A. Watkins, Jr., "Foliage Plants for Removing Indoor Air Pollution from Energy-Efficient Homes," *Economic Botany,* 1984, 38(2):224-228.

10. Wolverton, B.C., Space Biotechnology in Housing; NASA, National Space Technology Lab., January, 1986

11. Wood, R. A., et al. Study of Absorption of VOCs by Commonly Used Indoor Plants, *Proceedings: Indoor Air '99,* 1999, Vol. 2:690-694. (Australia).

Article 17

Pl. 1.Aeglonema

Pl. 2.Sansevieria

Pl. 3.Chrysanthemum

Pl. 4.Dracena

18

Occurrence of Fungal Biopollutants During Micropropagation of *Ficus religiosa* L.

Chitra Arya

Biopollutants like fungi, yeast and bacteria in tissue culture labs and diseases in greenhouse and nursery production areas are continue to cause and spread diseases. Their presence in environment may pose threat to plants animals and human beings. Fungi constitute major share of biopollutants as well as contaminant present in our atmosphere. Usually they reproduce by sexual and asexual means and their spores as well as conidia form component of Aerospora. Fungal spores may cause diseases and biodeteriora-tion of organic materials. Gregory (1973) recorded spread of fungi and bacteria by the action of wind and rain splash. In tropical and subtropical climate diseased plants can act as sources of airbone bio-pollution. These propagules may cause plant diseases and even allergy to human beings.

Apical and axillary buds of nodal explants were used. Bud breaking and sprouting took place on MS medium in 3-5 days. After 5 days fungal growth was observed near inoculated explants. 10% explants showed the growth of *Fusarium oxysporum* Schlecht. And 7% were infected with *Thielaviopsis* state of *Ceratocystis paradoxa*. These infected explants survived for 15 days. The healthy explants were transferred for multiple shoot induction on MS medium containing BA (1.5 mgl^{-1}) and ADS (1.5 mgl^{-1}). Within 2-days fungal biopollutants contaminated 30% of the flasks and growth of these fungi caused death of explants within 5 days. Certain fungi isolated inculded *Aspergillus flavus, A. niger, A. fumigatus, Alternaria infectoria, Cladosporium oxysporum, Curvularia lunata, Drechslera hawaiiensis, Fusarium oxysporum, Eurotium* sp. *Monascus ruber* and *Phialophora hoffmannii.*

Introduction

Air spora forms a normal component of the earth's atmosphere. Aerobiological studies have been gaining prominence due to their applications in various fields including clinical allergy. These studies are helpful in assessing the deterioration and managment of environment. Role of fungal bio pollulants have been emphesized in ocurraenc of plant and animal diseases These form an important component of aeroallergens which include pollen grains fungal spores, and fungal mycelium, also sometimes house dust and mites. In general these occur in domestic environment. In comparision to fields or village atmosphere the concentration of bio-particles is many times more in urban atmosphere. Studies have already shown their presence in large numbers in places like libraries (Kowalik 1980, Srivastava 1991, Singh and Tandon 1991, Strzwlezyk & Leznicka 1981), museums (Shah *et al.* 1996, Arya *et al.* 2001) and hospitals (Spieksma 1980). Extensive studies are lacking in tissue culture operations. Present paper records occurance of these pollutants during micropropagation of pipal tree (*Ficus religiosa*).

A variety of factors contribute to the contamination responsible for reduced multiplication rates, reduced rooting rates, and plant death in plant cell culture. These include ineffective methods for surface sterilization of the primary explant used in stage I, improper sterilization of media, culture vessels, or instruments used in plant tissue culture, improper handling of sterile plant material, or ineffective methods for detection of contaminants in plant cell cultures. Contaminants commonly found include bacteria, fungi, yeasts, thrips and mites. The most common yeast species isolated from contaminated plant tissue included *Candida* and *Rhodotorulla*, the most common fungi are *Fusarium, Aspergillus and Cladosporium* (Leifert and Waits 1990 & 1991). Most yeast and fungi grow well on plant cell culture media. A rapid spread of fungal or yeast contamination may be due to an infestation of either thrips or mites. Thrips and mites result in little direct damage to the plant tissue, but can serve as vectors for spreading contaminants throughout the culture room (Leifert and Waites 1990).

There are several ways to control contamination, but determining the source of contamination and the type of contamination is necessary to choose the best methods. First there should be an effective detection and indexing program to screen all tissue that is brought into the lab. Second, proper ascepetic techniques and handling of the media should be used. Finally, use of antibiotics and anti-fungal agents in the culture medium has proven to control contamination.

The Peepal tree, *Ficus religiosa* Linn., belongs to family Moraceae. It is one of the best known trees of India. It is planted in villages near the temples. The tree is 25 to 45 m high. The leaves and young branches are smooth and more or less shining, the leaves are some what leathery, broadly oval in shape suddenly narrowed at the apex, the base is heart shaped, the stalk of the leaf is long as the tailed apex. *F. religiosa* is a fast growing fuel wood tree of Indian forest (Santapau 1981). The studies were conducted to study the association of fungal pollutant with explants or internal contamination during micropropagation. The internal contamination may be due to presence of endophytes in the plants (Santos *et al*. 2003)

Materials and Methods

Young shoots were collected from a mature tree of *F. religiosa* growing in the Botanical garden of M.S. University of Baroda. These were cut into single node expants after the leaves were removed. The explants were washed under running tap water for 10 to 15 min., cleaned with a mild detergent and rinsed thoroughly with distilled water. Surface sterilization of these explants was carried out under asceptic conditions in laminar flow hood, where they were surface sterilized with 0.1% mercuric chloride, for 5 min. and then rinsed two to three times with sterile distilled water. MS medium containing 3% sucrose and 0.8% agar was used during the present studies. The pH of medium was adjusted to 5.8. The MS medium supplemented with different concentration of BA (2-5 mgl^{-1}) and IBA (0.05-2mgl^{-1}) was used for induction of bud break. The explants with induced bud break were transferred to MS medium supplemented with 1-2 mg 1^{-1} BA and 1-2 mg 1^{-1} ADS. For multiple shoots induction various growth regulators were used (Deshpande *et al.* 1998).

The organisms responsible for infestation of explants and other contamination were isolated, purified by single spore culture method and maintained on potato dextrose agar medium. Fungi were stained with lectophenol cotton blue (Staples, 1973). These were identified on the basis of morphological characters. Cultures were sent to IARI New Delhi for final confirmation.

Results and Discussion

After inoculation of explants in MS medium growth of two fungi was observed near the inoculated explants in a number of flasks. Ten per cent explants showed white cottony growth of *Fusarium oxysporum* Schlecht. (Plate 1, Photo B) and 7% explants were infected with *Thielaviopsis* state of *Ceratocystis paradoxa* which showed black thick myceilal growth near the explants (Plate 1, Photo D) . These dieseased explants surrived for 15 days.

The two bipollutants are important pathogens of a number of economic important plants (Bilgrami *ct al.* 1979). Their occurr-ence on this plant is new to the Science. Certain other fungal bipollutants were also found on MS medium containing flasks. These fungal contaminats may be saprophytic or parasitic. After one week, the healthy explants were died due to growth of fungal contaminants. Isolated fungi included *Aspergillus flavus, A. niger, A. fumigatus, Alternaria infectoria, Cladosporium oxysporum, Curvularia lunata, Drechslera hawaiiensis, Fusarium oxysporum, Eurotium sp. Monascus ruber and Phialophora hoffmannii* (Plate 1C, Plate 2 Photo A,B,C).

Early detection of fungal pathogens in plant material causing inhibition of growth during micropropagation is essential for prevention of spread of contamination. Micropropagation of plant tissue culture through apical and axillary buds of nodal explants or meristem tip culture does not always yield pathogen free plants (Wang 1985). Indexing systems are developed to prevent losses due to other diseases, such as vascular wilt of carnation (caused by *Fusarium oxysporum* f. sp. *dianthi*), carnation bacterial wilt (by *Pseudomonas coryophyilli*), Verticillium wilt of Geranium (*Verticillium albo-atrum*) (Raju and Olson 1985). Therefore, plant-indexing programs for viruses, bacteria and fungi should be implemented at various stages of micro-propagation. An effective indexing program may include the following:

1. Stock plants should be examined for symptoms of pathogens and the presence of pests. Infected plant material should be avoided.
2. Primary explants used to initiate plant cell cultures should be tested for the presence of viruses, bacteria and fungal contaminants. All infected material should be discarded.
3. Once the stock cultures are stablished and actively growing, cultures should be periodically examined for mites and thrips and indexed for the presence of viruses, bacteria and latent fungi. Several methods have been described for the detection of bacterial and fungal contamination in plant tissue. One effective method Enzyme Linked Immunosorbent Assays (ELISA) has been used for the detection and identification of plant viruses. The virus can be eliminated by culturing the meristem tip and raising this plant artifically in a tissue culture medium in the laboratory (Kolpmeyer 2003).

Testing for contamination, that may have occurred at some point in any operation can be done by transfer of suspected materials to the nutrient solution optimal for fungal or bacterial growth or potato dextrose medium and made to incubate for 24h at 37°C. Potato dextrose medium liquid or as agar plates is suitable for detection of bacteria, yeast and fungi (Klopmeyer 2003). Host range of *Peranospora atta* which is causing downy mildew of *Psyllium* spp. was detected by tissue culture techniques.

The spread of fungal and bacterial contaminats can also be controlled through improved ascepetic techniques and proper handling of the culture medium. To avoid bacterial and fungal growth, explants are disinfected before they are used to establish *in vitro* cultures. The disinfectants most widely used and their concentrations in the solution are given in table 1.

Plant tissue culture media are generally sterilized by autoclaving at 121°C and 15 psi. The time required for sterilization depends upon the volume of the medium. Several medium components are considered thermo-labile and should not be autoclaved. Stock solutions of the heat labile components are prepared and filter-sterilized through a 0.22 µm filter into a sterile container. The filtrate is aseptically added to the culture medium, which has been autoclaved and allowed to cool to approximately 35-45°C. The medium is then dispensed under sterile conditions. Bacterial contamination of "clean" cultures with *Bacillus*, which can produce alcohol-and heat resistant spores, has been reported (Boxus and Terzi 1987& 1988). The spread of this is typically the result of inefficient sterilization of instruments used for the handling of plant tissue. Sterilization of instruments is done in a heat source (e.g. flame, infra red or glass-bead sterilizer).

Disinfection of contaminated cultures is often difficult to accomplish due to the diversity of organisms present. Antibiotics and antifungal chemicals are routinely used to control contamina-tion. To be effective in plant tissue culture, the antibiotic or antifungal should be soluble and stable in the culture medium. It should also be effective when used in combination and have a broad spectrum of reactivity with minimal phytotoxic effects (Gilburt 1991 and Razdan 2003). Some of the antibiotics and antifungals routinely used in plant tissue culture are included in table 2.

Detection of pathogens and bio contaminants of plants and plant cell cultures is certainly a unmanageable task, but one that requires extra effort is Indexing and early detection programs, which will help to adopt various aseptic techniques, and to prevent or manage contamination in lab, green house, or nursery (USDA 2002).

REFERENCES

Arya, A., Shah A.R. and Sadasivan S. (2001) Indoor aeromycoflora of Baroda museum And deterioration of Egyptian mummy. Curr. Sci. 81(7): 793-799.

Bilgrami, K.S., Jamaluddin and Rijvi M.A. (1979). Fungi of India Vol. 1 Today and Tomarrow's Prints and Publishers, New Delhi 464pp.

Boxus, P.H. and Terzi J.M. (1987) Acta Horticulturae, 212:91.

Boxus, P.H. and Terzi J.M. (1988) Acta Horticulturae, 215:189.

Desphande, S.R., Josekutty, P.C. and Prathapasenan, G. (1998). Plant regeneration from axillary buds of a mature tree of *Ficus religiosa*. Plant Cell Reports. 17:571-573.

Gilburt J.E. (1991) Ann. Appl. Biol., 119:113.

Gregory, P.H. (1973) Microbiology of atmosphere(2) Leonard Hill Books Aylesbury Bucks U.K. 377p.

Klopmeyer M. (2003) Indexing for diseases Flora Culture International, p. 16-17.

Kowalik, R. (1980) Microbioradation of Library Materials, Part-II. Microbiodegradation of basic organic materials, Ch. IV. Retaurator, 4:135-291.

Leifert, C. and Waites W.M. (1990). J. Applied Bacteriology, 69:471.

Leifert, C., and Waites W.M. (1991). World J. Micro and Biotech. 7:452.

Niedz, Randall P. (1998). Using isothiazolone biocides to control microbiol and fungal contaminants in plant tissue cultures. Hort. Technology. 8(4): 598-601.

Raju, B.C. and Olson, C.J. (1985). Indexing system for producing clean stock for diseases control in commercial floriculture. Plant Dis. 69, 189.

Razdan, M.K. (2003). Introduction to plant tissue culture. Oxford & IBH publishing Co. Pvt. Ltd. New Delhi. pp375.

Santapaua, H. (1981) Common Trees Pub. National Book Trust, India, New Delhi. 118pp.

Santos, R.M.G., Rodrigues-Fo E., Rocha, W.C. and Teixeira, M.F.S. (2003) Endophytic Fungi from Melia Azedarch, World J. Microbiol. Biotech. 19:767-770

Shah, N.R.(1990) Conservation of a wooden plaque. Con. of Cul. Prop. in India, New Delhi, 28:26-27.

Shah, N.R. Arya, A., Shah, A.R. and Bhowmik, S.K.(1996) A study of atmospheric Sci. (eds) V. Rai, M.L. Naik, C. Manoharachary, School of Life Sci. Pt. RaviShankar Shukla Univ. Raipur pp 189-196

Singh, R.S. and Tandon, O.P. (1991) A mycological analysis of the air in the Bharat Kala Bhavan. In "Bio. Det. Of Cul. Prop". (Eds. Agrawal, O.P. & Dhawan, S.) MacMillan India Ltd., New Delhi, 405-411.

Spieksma, F.T.M. (1980). Importance of Aerobiological Studies for the Prediction of Human Diseases. Aerobiol. Symp. Munich. 307-315p.

Srivastava, A.K. (1991) On the aeromycology of *Chaetomium* in Lucknow. In, "Biodet. of Cul. Prop. (Eds. Aggarwal, O.P. & Dhawan, S.) MacMillan India Ltd., New Delhi, 397-404.

Staples, D.G. (1973). An Introduction to Microbiology. Pub. by Macmillan Education Ltd. 193pp.

Strzewlczyk A.B. and Leznicka S.L. (1981) The role of fungi and bacteria in consolidation of books., Int. Biodet. Bull. 17 (2):57-67.

Wang, P.J. (1985). I.A.P.T.C. News letter. 46:2.

USDA Agricultural research Service (2002) Control of *in vitro* contamination of explants from greenhouse and field grown trees. *In vitro* Cellular and Development Biology. In http://www.nps.ars.usda.gov.

Table. 1 : Commonly used disinfectant for plant tissue culture

	Disinfectant	*Concentration (%)*	*Exposure (Min.)*
1.	Sodium hypochlorite	0.5-5	5-30
2.	Hydrogen peroxide	3-12	5-15
3.	Ethyl alcohol	70-95	0.1-5.0
4.	Silver nitrate	1	5-30
5.	Mercuric chloride	0.1-1.0	2-10
6.	Benzalkonium chloride	0.01-0.1	5-20

Table 2. Commonly used Antibiotics/Anti-fungal compounds in plant tissue culture (Niedz 1988)

S.No.	*Antibiotics*	*Toxicity to microbes μg/ml*
1.	Carbenicillin	500
2.	Cefotaxime	90
3.	Chloramphenicol	128
4.	Erythromycin	60
5.	Gentamycin sulfate	50
6.	Penicillin G potassium	70
7.	Penicillin G sodium	87
8.	Streptomycin Sulfate	50
9.	Vancomycin	5
10.	Amphotericin B	2.5
11.	Nystatin	50
12.	Pentachloronitrobenezene	20
13.	Thiabendazole	35
14.	Isothiazolone (Biocides)	50

Plate 1.

Photo A. Healthy shoots of *Ficus religiosa* growing in MS medium

Photo B. Explants showing growth of *Fusarium oxysporum.*

Photo C. Growth of *A. flavus* associated with explants.

Photo D. Growth of black coloured mycelium of *Thielaviopsis* state of *Ceratocystis paradoxa.*

Plate 2.

Photo A & C. Growth of *F. oxysporum* in one of the explant

Photo B. Bacterial growth near one explant and growth of *Alternaria infectoria* near another explant.

Pl.1A. Healthy shoots of Ficus religiosa growing in MS medium

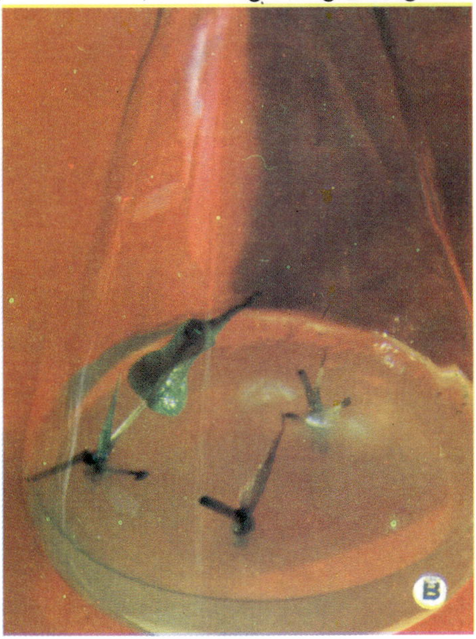

B. Explants showing growth of Fusarium oxysporum

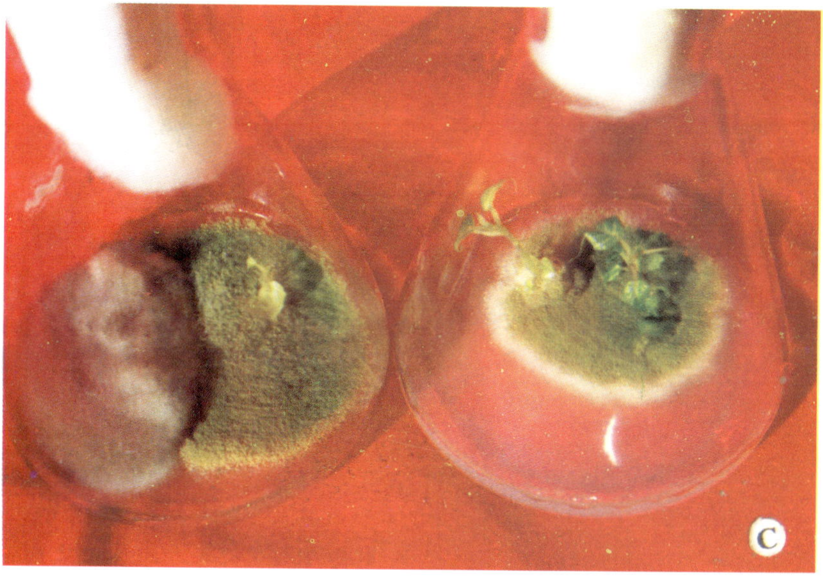

C. Growth of A. flavus associated with explants.

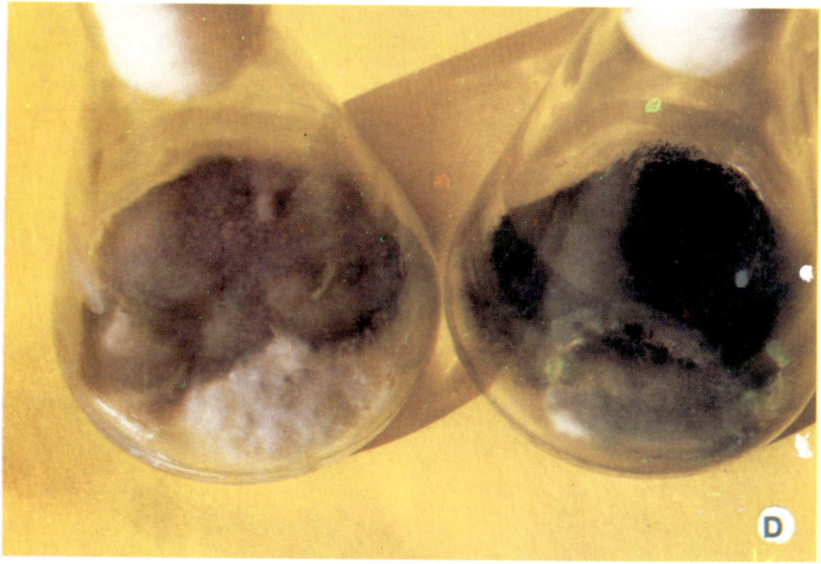

D. Growth of black coloured mycelium of Thielaviopsis state of Ceratocystis paradoxa.

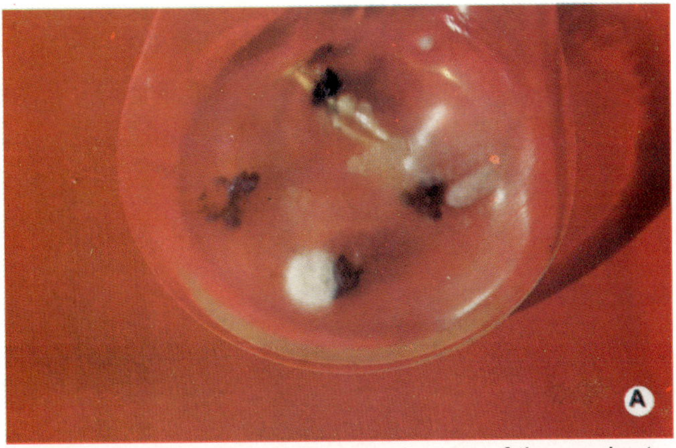

Pl.2. A. Growth of F. oxysporum in one of the explants.

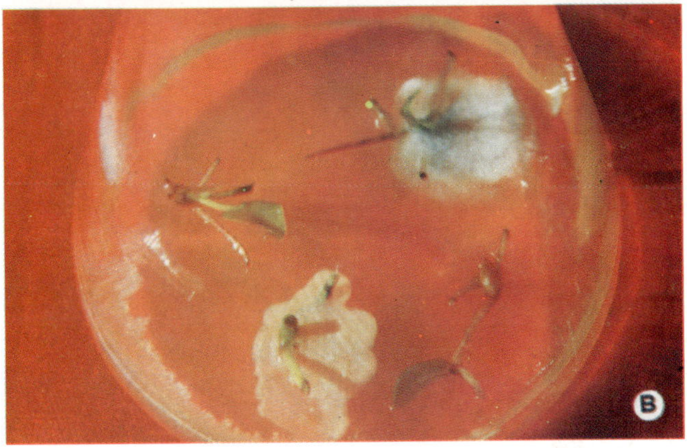

B. Bacterial growth near one explant and growth of Alternaria infectoria near another explants.

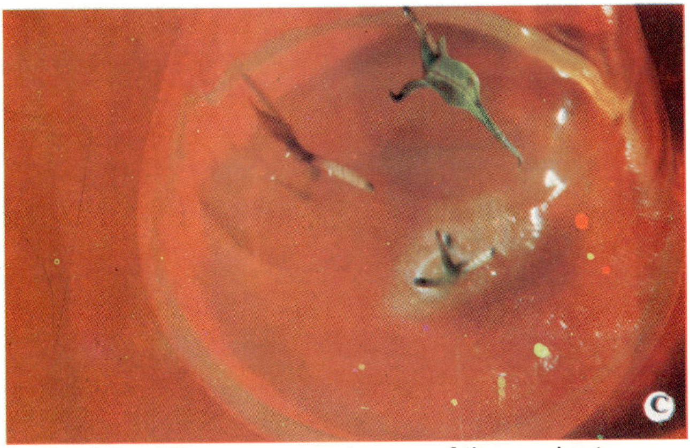

C. Growth of F. oxysporum in one of the explants.

19

Role of Vegetation in Making Cities Better Liven up

Yogesh T. Jasrai and P. S. Sisodia

Vegetation play an effective role in the urban environment, supporting many fundamental subsystems like hydrological cycles, nutrients cycles, atmospheric gas balance etc. However, increasing population and the rapid urbanization process are converting more and more green spaces into impermeable hard concrete jungles. Such implications deprive the city of green spaces and generate stress in our life. The urban areas also experience water scarcity, air pollution; heat islands etc apart from similar such problems like traffic congestion and vehicular pollution. Number of studies undertaken in this direction suggested that the development of green areas improves the urban environmental conditions. There could be number of attempts in this direction to increase the green spaces in the urban areas such as urban forestry, silviculture, afforestation, social forestry with the aim of improving the environmental conditions.

The golden corridor (Ahmedabad to Vapi) has been lined up with scores of small and large scale industries. Over the years, Vadodara has also witnessed establishment of medium and large scale industries with great strides in economic field. The city has giant industrial complexes and public undertakings like Gujarat Refinery, Indian Petro-chemicals, Gujarat State Fertilizers and Chemicals, Alembic Pharmaceuticals, Heavy

Water Project, Oil and Natural Gas Commission to name few of them. The present document deals with the role of trees in making cities liven up. In our survey total 179 tree species were found in Vadodara, of which 35 plant species are very important with their ability to control air pollution.

Key words: Vadodara, trees, urban environment

Introduction

Several factors are responsible for environmental pollution, chief among these factors are build up of CO_2 or other greenhouse gases in the atmosphere and a host of man made elements causing toxic wastes and ozone depletion. Air pollution and anthropogenic disturbances have caused destruction of plant and animal natural habitats to varying degrees. This rapid growth rate of many cities, combined with their huge population base, is pushing the cities to unprecedented sizes. These processes have modified the natural features of a city and its surroundings (geography, topography and climate) through following main ways: **i**.the conversion of agriculture land to urban uses, **ii**.the extraction and depletion of natural resources. **iii**. the disposal of wastes in the urban set up. As the cities expand, prime agricultural land and habitats such as wetlands and forests in and around the city get transformed into land for housing, roads and industry. Increasing industrial develop-mental activities accelerate these further due to which many of the plant species become rare. Losses of biological diversity are now significant and these could affect the future well being of human life. Sustainable use of biodiversity is therefore a matter of paramount importance. To develop biodiversity sustainably, one must know the species present in an ecosystem and their interdependence including causes of their disturbance. It is found that the number of such activities does bring more green spaces, however attempts on the integration of trees as an element of urban landscape are missing. Such an attempt would deliver functionally more effective and aesthetically pleasing environment. This requires many aspects to be considered such as ownerships, soil types, hydrology, topography, micro and macro climatic conditions, size and nature of the city, natural vegetation, type of industries etc.

The Vadodara city generally known as Garden city of Gujarat is also known as cultural capital of Gujarat. It comprises an area of about 108.22 km^2 and is situated on both the banks of the river Vishwamitri. It lies between 22° 17' 59" N latitude and 73°15' 18" E longitude. It is almost a plain area, beautifully planned city and a district place in the Gujarat State. The climate of the Vadodara city is markedly periodic and is characterized by a dry and increasingly hot summer from March to June, dry and cold winter from November to February and a warm monsoon from July to September.

Green spaces in the urban set up

The integrated system of human components and the biophysical variables (environment) of the city are commonly known as the urban ecosystem. The relationships between these two components are extremely complex and always conflicting with each other. The cities are expanding in its size at the expense of the nature (biophysical variables). The green spaces (trees, lawns/parks, forest and cultivated land) are the only potential biophysical elements to sustain our city. According to American Forestry Association (AFA), one city tree can provide over 57,000 $ worth of air conditioning, erosion, storm water control, wild life shelter and also air pollution control over 50 years of its life span. In fact such spaces are the lungs of the city, picking polluted air and releasing fresh and good air.

The ever-increasing demands for building and paving in the urban area impaires physical environment to the extent that the spatial patterns are more fragmented and city becomes less lively in nature. The gap between the urban man and the nature get widened. The green spaces are the potential design elements (apart from its ecological/environmental benefits) which are capable of bringing together the entire city through defining, reinforcing and creating various spaces in different levels (micro level to macro level). The potential use of the trees in shaping and making our cities more liven up remain unperceived one. As an animal, man always relates himself empathically to his environment. Many social scientist proved that introducing the nature in the form of vegetations, wildlife, soil and water in significant quantity is very close to the natural living and working place which will improve the community health and the working efficiency of individuals in the city.

Present work in this direction towards control of air pollution in the urban ecosystem (through urban agriculture, social forestry, urban forestry, silviculture, aforestation, urban farming) apart from the marketable returns of the plantation emphasize on the air pollution resistance of tree species in the city. To get the quick and faster results, introduction of single species or exotic plants in large extent *(Eucalyptus, Casuarina equisetifolia),* may create many problems in the urban area, such as,

i. Loss of biodiversity
ii. Altering basic cyclic pattern of the local ecosystem - hydrological cycle, nutrient cycle
iii. Some species do not allow the other species to grow near by (allelopathy) so that it slowly replaces the local species
iv. Monoculture - susceptible for environmental problems such as being prone to climatic change and diseases
v. Impoverishment/nutrients imbalance of the soil due to over consumption of the particular minerals and nutrients.

The balance between the socio-economic development of the city and the threshold limits of its biophysical variables are inevitable to support the man's biological and physical needs to continue the existence. We often fail to integrate the green spaces with our city's functional systems. Because of our incompetence in handling this element in the urban space, urban tree remains impediment to various urban *activities* and stands aloof. In fact, this natural element needs to be integrated in such a way that it should support the efficient function and healthy growth of the urban area.

Design aspects of the green spaces

Urban trees are the powerful symbols (architectural objects), which can produce poetry or even inspire depending on the way they are handled. The arrangement, spacing, location and type of species must be identified individually to meet the functional requirements of the each urban space. Some of the important design implications to use the green spaces as design elements in the urban area are

i. Plantation of some of the plant species which are resistant to air pollution.

ii. Trees should be used in such a way that it should convey a scale that is sympathetic to the nature of the function which is associated with each space.

iii. Trees should express the particular site wherever it is planted, through its arrangement in terms of unique pattern, foliage and form.

iv. Using single species in a group to express the collective impact of homogeneity of texture, pattern, light and shade than an individual tree.

v. The consistency between tree pattern and surroundings can be achieved by geometry or by subtle forms.

For these criteria, the choice of the right tree species is a very difficult task. We have surveyed the whole city and identified a total of 179 tree species of which 35 tree species are very important for their ability to control air pollution.

Table-1. Tree species with ability to purify polluted air.

Botanical name	Botanical name
Polyalthia longifolia	*Samanea saman*
Thespesia populnea	*Anogeissus sericea*
Ceiba pentandra	*Eucalyptus globulus*
Guazuma ulmifolia	*Lagerstroemia speciosa*
Ailanthus excelsa	*Alangium salvifolium*
Azadirachta indica	*Anthocephalus indicus*
Butea monosperma	*Manilkara hexandra*
Dalbergia latifolia	*Salvadora persica*
Dalbergia sissoo	*Cordia dichotoma*

Botanical name	Botanical name
Pongamia pinnata	*Kigelia pinnata*
Bauhinia purpurea	*Gmelina arborea*
Cassia fistula	*Tectona grandis*
Cassia siamea	*Emblica officinalis*
Tamarindus indica	*Putranjiva roxburghii*
Acacia auriculiformis	*Ficus benghalensis*
Acacia nilotica	*Ficus religiosa*
Albizzia lebbeck	*Streblus asper*
Casuarina equisetifolia	

Trees and urban air pollution

Trees play an invaluable role in reducing man made urban air pollution and improve human health through,

i. The direct and indirect benefits of trees for urban air quality and improving quality of life.

ii. Trees reduce the air pollution by removal of obnoxious gases and particulates from the air through stomatal movement and deposition.

iii. Trees also help to slow global warming, mostly attributed to the increasing levels of greenhouse gases, specially CO_2 caused by fossil fuel combustion and even deforestation.

iv. Trees are one of the most effective mechanisms for cleaning the air of contaminants and for supplying oxygen.

v. Trees reduce ambient temperature in three ways

   a. use of solar energy for photosynthesis.

   b. provide shade and shelter

   c. evapotranspiration to cool themselves and the surrounding air.

vi. Trees also reduce storm water run-off, erosion, flooding and water pollution.

vii. Trees also reduce urban noise, which has been associated with a number of adverse health effects.

Article 19

Pl. 1.Role of such trees for making cities better liven up.

A.Butea monosperma

B.Manilkara hexandra

C.Azadirachta indica

D.Acacia nilotica

E.Thespesia populena

Pl. 2.Role of such trees for making cities better liven up.

A.Ficus benghalensis

B.Tectona grandis

C.Anogeissus sericea

D.Mimusops elengi

viii. As per the rough estimates the tree that lives for 50 years help in generating

a. Rs. 5.3 lakh worth of oxygen.

b. Rs. 6.4 lakh worth of soil fertility.

c. Rs. 6.4 lakh worth of soil erosion control.

d. Rs. 10.5 lakh worth of air pollution control.

e. Rs. 5.3 lakh worth of shelter for birds and animals.

So, when one tree falls or felled the city's net loss is worth more than Rs. 33 lakhs.

REFERENCE

Sahni, K.C. (1998) The book of Indian trees, BNHS, Bombay.

Shah, G.L. (1978) Flora of Gujarat State (Vol. 1 & 2) Sardar Patel University, Vallabh Vidyanagar.

Anonymous. (2000) Guidelines for developing green belts, Central Pollution Control Board, New Delhi.

Saha, D. (1998) Tolerance levels of certain tree species towards industrial air Pollution, Ph.D. Thesis submitted to The Maharaja Sayajirao University of Baroda, Vadodara.

20

Pollution in the City of Taj : Some Measures for Reduction of Air Pollution

S.B. Rao, M. Radha Krishna, Ranjit Singh, C. Patvardhan

Different types of Pollution viz. Air Pollution, Water Pollution, Noise Pollution, Land Pollution and Radiation Pollution affect human life very much. A very serious complicating factor towards the failure in curbing the pollution menace is the apathy of the society-at-large towards this problem. This apathy, which is refered to as attitude pollution, results in use of polluting vechicles neglecting the harm they cause in pursuit of economic gains for the self. They even forget that the harmful effects of pollution are borne by everbody including themselves.

The historical city of Agra has a number of monuments and World Heritage buildings. Therefore, attention is also being paid to protect these valuable assets from the ill effects of Air Pollution. In this view, the Central Pollution Control Board (CPCB) has established an office in Agra to monitor quality of air. The pollutants they measure are nitrogen di-oxide (NO_2), Sulphur di-oxide (SO_2) and suspended particulate matter (SPM). The Supreme Court has banned several industries after going through the reports submitted by CPCB. From a recent

CPCB report it is understood that Agra is one of the 10 most polluted cities in India.

Not much work has been reported regarding the vehicular pollution in Agra resulting from burgeoning number of vehicles in the last few years. In this paper, an attempt has been made to study the various parameters pertaining to vehicluar traffic pollution at observation sites set up at the major traffic intersections of Agra City. The data collected show that the pollution resulting from vehicular traffic has already reached high levels. The situation will continue to become worse because of growth in human and vehicular population. Further to this, the emissions from founderies of Agra aggravate the situation.

A number of strategies for the reduction of the air pollution caused by vehicular emission and emissions from foundries are proposed and briefly discussed. It is imperative that such studies be carried out in a more elaborate manner. Further, immediate measures are required to ensure that situation is brought under control. Some immediately feasible measures are identified and highlighted for this purpose. Recognizing the importance of attitude pollution referred above, adequate importance is expected by user education in changing attitudes toward the problems of pollution in tackling the menace.

1. Introduction

The reports of the environmental pollution panel of US President Science Advisory Committee (1965) define environmental pollution as unfavourable alteration of our surroundigs, wholly or largely as a by-product of man's actions through direct or indirect effects of changes in energy patterns, radiation levels, chemical or physical constitution and abundance of organisms. The various types of pollution are—Air Pollution, Land Pollution, Water Pollution, Radiation Pollution, Noise Pollution. Engineers Joint Council defines Air Pollution as the presence in the outdoor atmosphere of one or more contaminats, such as dust, fumes, gas, mist, odor, smoke or vapour in quantities for such duration so as to be injurious to human, plant or animal life or to property or which unreasonably interfere with the comfortable enjoyment of life and property.

The five most common effects of air pollution are reduction in visibility, economic damage to property, annoyance to humans senses, damage to health, substantive changes in the ecology of the natural environment. The composition of clean, dry air may indicate presence of compounds that are considered to be pollutants. Some of them are NO_2, O_3, SO_2,CO and NH_3. Though their concentrations are very low in unpolluted air, under polluted conditions they are generally increased and affect the human life [1,2,3,4] as given below.

Table 1 : Effect of Air Pollutants

S.No.	*Pollutant Species*	*Primary Effects*
1.	Carbon monoxide	Toxic, Reduces O_2 carrying capacity of blood.
2.	Hydrocarbons	Depends on particular composition, can be relatively inert (CH_4), photo-chemical smog precursors (reactive HC), toxic (carcinogens)
3.	Oxides of Nitrogen	Toxic, photochemical smog precursor, reduction of visibility
4.	Smoke, Particulates	Visibility reduction, plume visibility, possible carriers of toxic mate-rials, nucleation sites, possible weather modification
5.	Oxides of Sulphur	Toxic, aerosol formation
6.	Aldehydes	Irritants, odorants, photochemical smog precursors
7.	Metals (Mn, V, Na, P, etc)	Toxic, atmospheric reactions
8.	S-Compounds (H_2S etc)	Toxic, odorants

In this paper, an attempt has been made to study the various parameters pertaining to vehicular traffic pollution at observation sites set up at the major traffic intersections of Agra City and observe the attitude of the vehicle owners, vehicle users. The data collected show that the pollution resulting from vehicular traffic has already reached high levels and urgent measures are required to deal with the problem. A brief study of the emissions from conventional foundries using the cupolas is also carried out.

The rest of the paper is organised as follows. In section 2, the air pollution due to automotive emissions and the standards for safe vehicular emissions and pollution levles as per Motor vehicle Act are presented. In section 3, some observations regaiding the vehicular and human population are presented. In section 4, various approaches for reduction of air pollution and some measures already taken to reduce air pollution in Agra are discussed and a number of measures that can be taken to reduce air pollution in Agra are discussed and a number of measures that can be taken at district level and Government level are suggested. Finally, in section 5, the conclusions of the present work have been presented along with pointers for future work.

2. Automotive Emissions And Air Pollution

Vehicle population in India has roughly tripled since 1990. Automotive emissions in winter are very dangerous as the air is still and creeps along the ground enveloping us in poisonous shroud. More than 40,000 people die prematurely every year in India because of air pollution, says a World Bank Report 1996.

Pollution Standards in India

The motor Vehicle Act 1939; modified by Motor Vehicle (Amendment) Act, 1982, empowers state governments to adopt suitable measures for controlling vehicular exhaust emissions. Table 2.1 lists the standards specified by Motor Vehicle Act, 1982 in this regard.

Table 2.1: Vehicle Emission Standards (M.V. Act-1982)

S. No.	*Vehicle Condition*	*Petrol Driven Vehicles (% CO)*	*Diesel Driven Vehicles Hatridge Smoke Unit*
1.	New Vehicle	3.5	65
2.	5 Years old or completed 8000 Km.	4.5	75

Ambient Air Quality Standards

The Central Pollution Control Board (CPCB) in collaboration with the State Pollution Control Boards has established a National Ambient Air Quality Monitoring network consisting of 290 stations in 92 cities in India under Air Act, 1981, Uttar Pradesh has 38 Stations with one such center at. Agra. In the year 1994, under section 16 (2)(h) of the Air Act (1981), CPCB laid down and notified the air quality standards, which are as given in Table 2.2.

Table 2.2 : Ambient Air Quality Standards

Pollution	*Residential Area*	*Industrial Area*
Carbon Monoxide (CO) mg/m^3	2.00	2.00
Hydrocarbons (HC) PPM	200	200
SO_2	30-60	40-80
SPM	70-140	180-360

3. Measurement Of Air Pollution

Agra lies 200 Kms. South of National Capital Delhi on the level and fertile Gangetic Plain which is furrowed by several rivers, the most important of which is the Yamuna. Agra is situated on its West bank. The city is 169 m above sea level and covers 65 Sq. Kms.

In the past few years, the population and number of vehicles in Agra has risen as given in Table 3.1.

Table 3.1 : Rise in Vehicle & Human Population

Vehicle Type	31.3.95	31.3.97	31.3.98	31.3.99	31.3.00	31.3.01	31.3.02
Car/4wheeler	10,418	11,981	13,778	15,845	18,222	21,142	24,736
2 Wheelers	1,58,512	1,82,289	2,09,632	2,41,007	2,77,238	31,876	36,984
Population (Lakhs)	**12.088**	**12.333**	**12.572**	**12.813**	**13.055**	**13.320**	**13.591**

In table 3.1 it can be observed that there has been a 15% increse in vehicular population per annum, whereas the human population growth is 2% per annum.

Central Pollution Control Board (CPCB) office in Agra

measures nitrogen di-oxide (NO_2), Sulphur di-oxide (SO_2) and suspended particulate matter (SPM) at various locations of Agra. Presently no other government agency has paid attention to the principal pollutants from the automotive emissions i.e. Carbon Monoxide (CO) and Unburnt Hydrocarbons (UHC). Therefore in this study all the pollutants in the air have been measured and the data recorded is presented.

3.1 Measurement sites in Agra city

The first spot selected for the measurement of Air Pollution is Poiyaghat Road near Dairy Bagh, where the vehicular traffic is extremely less. The Air Pollution on this spot is therefore taken as reference point and the pollution level on this spot forms the "target" for reducation in pollution level of all other seven spots, situated at the four corners of the city. Air Pollution has been measured at places having a number of industries and heavy traffic connecting Agra to other important cities of the country.

3.2 Experimental Data

The pollution measuring instruments were taken to measure the Air pollution at all the Eight spots of the city. These spots were selected on the basis of high traffic intensity and the area where most of the Industries are situated. The measurement of emissions is reported in table 3.2.

Table 3.2 : Measurement of Air Pollution

Pollutant	*Poiya Ghat*	*Sikandra*	*Ram Bagh*	*Bijlighar*	*Bhagwan Talkies*	*Pratappura*	*Nunhai*	*Taj Mahal*
CO	0.97	2.08	2.06	2.70	2.84	2.78	2.57	1.90
UHC	140	220	220	230	230	220	240	195
SO_2	15	40	50	55	45	40	40	35
NO_2	15	40	50	55	45	40	40	35
SPM	50	210	235	240	200	215	220	200

The concentration of CO is high (Premissible level 2.0 mg/m^3) in the area of Bijilighar, Bhagwan Talkies, Pratappura and Nunhai due to vehicular traffic of Two/Three wheelers.

From the above mesurement of pollutants it is clear that

the emission levels of hydro carbons (HC) are higher (Permisible level 200 ppm) in all the places except the Pioya Ghat Roads. The vehicular population (as from the data available) increasing @ 15% annually will increase the Air Pollution manifold. The situation will be further aggravated due to increase in population @ 2% in coming years. One of the locations, Bhagwan Talkies crossing has high volume of 2-3 wheeler traffic, trucks etc. Therefore, the concentration level of HC and CO are high. This is particularly alarming as there are a large number of residential colonies very close to this crossing on all the sides. This data indicates that measures should be taken to reduce the pollution level in the city immediately keeping future traffic trends in view.

In Nunhai, where most of the industries situated, all the pollutants are on high side. The emission levels of Coke-fired furnace, which also affect the ambient air quality are given in table 3.3.

Table 3.3 : Measurement of Air Pollution in Foundries.

Pollutant	*Permissible Level mg/m³*	*Coke Fired Furnace mg/m³*	*LDO fired Rotary Furnace mg/m³*
SO_2	350	600-750	88-90
SPM	150	1000-1800	35-40

From the above mesurement of the pollutants, it is clear that the emission level of coke-fired furnace is above the permissible limit. The use of coke in the furance also cause the depletion of the natural resources.

3.3 Attiude Pollution

While taking measurement of the pollutants at major location in the city, it is observed that the Auto-rickshaw operators take 7-8 commuters in auto for the sake of economic gains resulting in overloading of auto and the consequent pollution. Similar is the case with Tempo operators. Commuters also see their own econo-mic benefit as cost of transportion is shared by the increased number of commuters.

Some of the truck owners have their own way of working. As soon as the truck is purchased it is driven to a mechanic, who lets in more fuel. Therefore a 10 ton truck is modified so it can carry some 14 tons, Similarly, some of the bus owners get the number of seats enhanced after getting it passed for specific number of passengers.

In general, the vehicle owner also avoids to invest to get the pollution under control certificate but is forced to get it being mandatory as per as the Motor Vehicle act. Some of the owners of the polluting vehicles get the Pollutiuon Under Control certificate at some extra charge.

In brief, it is observed that the attitude of the vehicle owners or operators is centered towards their own economic gaius and they do not care about the amount of pollution their vehicle gene-rates which affects the society-at-large induding themselves. The proprietos of the. small scale industries also try to continue the production as and when possible in small quantities with some reasoning and excuses inspite of the orders to the cotontrary from the Honourable Court.

4. Strategies For Reduction Of Air Pollution In Agra City

4.1 Different Strategies

The nine different strategies commonly used to reduce the Air Pollution level are as given below:

i. Modification of engine design and operating conditions (Vehicle factor) [18].

ii. Traffic administration (Traffic factor).

iii. Educating vehicle users [9].

iv. Strict enforcement by Govt. and its departments

v. Enhancement of fuel quality & fuel supply

vi. Provision of Gas connection to individual industry at the earliest.

vii. Financial Support to the Research Organisation

viii. Technical Support to the Foundary Industries

ix. Financial Support to the Foundry Industries

Some of these strategies have already been attempted by vehicle manufacturers to some extent by the engine design modification or treatment of exhaust gas or exhaust emission control by fuel variation.

In Agra, the measures already in force and those that are suggested are discussed in sections 4.2 and 4.3.

4.2 Mesures taken in Agra

In Agra, under Indias Zero Emission Transport Programme, the US Agency for International Development (USAID) electric three-wheeler has been introduced on the road connecting tourists spots i.e. Taj Mahal to Agra Fort. Bajaj Auto Ltd. India and New Generation motors from US have collaborated and developed this auto-rickshaw. Such initatives assist in the long run and are very important. District Magistrate, Agra has banned tempos on M.G. Road. These measures indicate the seriousness with which the problems has been viewed by the District Administration and are Certainly contributing to reduce the increasing Pollution. However, as the experimental data presented in section 3 indicate, these measures are certainly insufficient in curbing this menace. There-fore, it is imperative that stronger and more effective measures be considered and implemented before the problem becomes unmangeable.

The CNG gas pipe line has been laid down for supply to individuals for melting the iron in various small scale industries.

4.3 Measures to be taken

The measures suggested are classified in two categories i.e. District Measures and Government Level Measures.

District Level Measures

1. Vehicle/car owners must be educated to become environmental friendly by maintaining their vehicle/cars properly and by driving them efficiently. This can be done through advertisement in local Newspapers, Radio, T.V. and display boards at major traffic intersections etc. Advertisements and local Newspaper, radio-talks etc. should put emphasis

on curbing the overloading of commercial vehicles plying on the city roads.

2. Implementing the CNG fuel in four metro cities has been troublesome due to lack of adequate number of CNG filling stations. This is to be avoided in Agra and use of CNG is to be encouraged.
3. On the basis of observation of traffic at Bhagwan talkies it is suggested that traffic going to Aligarh, Hathras etc. be diverted from Sikandara through a bridge at Poiya Ghat. The construction work should be initiated at the earliest and should be completed in specified time.
4. Use of high frequency mass transport system instead of small transport vehicles i.e. autos, tempos etc. on M.G. Road should be promoted.
5. On the basis of observation of traffic at Bhagwan talkies it is also suggested that use of Mughal Road and 100 ft. Road behind Jeewan Jyoti/Adan Bagh instead of Bhagwan Talkies-Poiya Ghat Road by the residents of the corresponding residential areas should be encouraged by creating adequate facillities like lighting, manned crossings to ensure orderly traffic etc.
6. Roads should be made wider so that mass transit system may ply easily. Mass transit system should ne enhanced considerably.
7. Vehicles without pollution control equipment i.e. catalytic converters etc. should be banned.
8. One-way traffic system should be introduced at places where congestion of traffic is usually observed.
9. The Air Pollution regulations should be strictly followed to reduce the pollution level.
10. There is a need to set up the Agra Pollution Control Committee to carry out Industrial/Vehicular Survey or census, complie and authentic database, analyze and project the future, stop adulteration at tanker-loading

points and petrol pumps and submit the report to district authorities form time to time.

11. Display boards showing the pollution level at few important crossings and the industrial area should be installed so as increase the awareness among the people.

Government Level Measures:

1. Advertisement in newspaper, radio, T.V. etc. should put emphasis on curbing the overloading of commercial vehicles and work for building up a Pollution Conscious Society. This can be achieved in the same way as population control. The population growth has been reduced from 2.5% in early 70s to 1.4% in late 90s by advertisements in TV and radio and extension programs.
2. Unleaded petrol should be promoted by keeping it cheaper than the leaded petrol.
3. Pollution control should be under a single Ministry/ umberlla to avoid confusion in working. This can be in the form of National Environment Protection Agency (NEPA) not only to control pollution but also to protect environment and coordinate the related matters within various government departments.
4. A tight time-frame program should be introduced within which lead must be discountinued in petrol, or at least limit to 0.1 grams per litre. Refineries should be required to trun out lead-free high octane fuel fit for use in all older vehicles: cars, scooters, mopeds, motorbikes, auto-rickshaws to reduce vehicular emissions.
5. In the interest of controlling vehicular emissions, the cost of converters should be spread equally on the cars, fitted or unfitted.
6. CNG users should be educated to use CNG kits manufactured by aprroved producers and to get it installed from authorized workshops and get it tested for safety every five years.
7. Government should ensure that the manufacturer in

different cities should provide training facillities to make the staff of the workshop/organization engaged in CNG conversion work capable and technically sound.

8. R&D efforts should be made to manufacture Electric driven vehicle that is highly effective to reduce air pollution.
9. Ban should be imposed on vehicles on the basis of engine performance instead of age of the vehicle.
10. CNG should be supplied through pipe line to individual industries at the earliest.
11. Financial support should be given to the industries to procure new equipment new technology, that are environment friendly.
12. The technical know-how/technical information sharing should be encouraged.
13. The research work being done in this area by Research/ Academic Institutes like P.P.D.C., a Government Organisation, D.E.I. (Deemed University), should be financially supported by the Goverment.

5. Conclusions

The air pollution in Agra can be reduced only when All the following agencies work together and collectively fight against the menace of Air Pollution:

* Auto manufacturers
* Traffic Control Administration
* Vehicle Owners/Users
* Govt. Department-Road Transport Authorities and Pollution Control Boards
* Fuel Manufacturers
* Industrialists & Institutions engaged in this research area

Scope Of Research

There is ample scope of conducting such studies in a more

elaborate manner. In general, the techniques available for melting the iron are:

1. InductionFurnace
2. Cokeless Furnace
3. Crucible Furnace
4. Rotary Furnace
5. Laser and Plasma Arc Furnace

Investigation for finding out the suitable iron melting technique, safeguarding the environment, should be taken up.

Further, immediate measures are required to be taken to ensure that the situation is brought under control.

REFRENCES

1. "Pllution from Automobile Engines and its Control-Combustion Generated Air Pollution", Prof. Natarajan. R., I.I.T. Chennai, 1989.
2. "Pollution from Automobile Engines and its Control-Introduction to Air Pollution", Dr. Srinivasa Rao, P., I.I.T. Chennai, 1989.
3. "Pollutioon from Automobile Engines and its Control-Automotive Emissions and Air Pollution", Dr. Srinivasa Rao, P., I.I.T. Chennai, 1989.
4. "Pollution from Automobile Engines and its Control-Emission Measuring Instrumentation". Prof. Durgaprasada Rao, ch., I.I.T., Chennai, 1989.
5. Pollution Control Acts & Rules with Amendments", Central Pollution Control Board, Delhi, 1989.
6. "Catalytic Converter System for Spark Ignition Engine Exhaust Emission Control-Design Development and Performance Evaluation", Rao, S.B., Ph.D. Thesis, IIT Delhi, 1995.
8. "Car tips for Clean Air", Sikrosky Robert, Pergee Books, New York, 1991
9. "Vehicular air pollution in Agra & some measures for its reduction", M.R. Krishna, Minor Project, M.Tech., Dayalbagh Educational Institute, May, 2001.
10. "Rotary Furnace: A quest for converting its potential into a cleaner, healthier planet", Ranjit Singh, Samyak Jain, M. Radha Krishna, Indian Journal of Air Pollution, Delhi, Vol. 2, No.2, September, 2002.

21

Waste Water Treatment : Removal of Dyes from Industrial Effluents

M.N. Ahmed and R.N. Ram (Late)

Adsorption plays a very important role in removing the waste as well as the toxic materials from the industrial effluents. The present study includes the removal of basic dyes (basic brown 4 & basic violet 2) from aqueous solution using basic alumina as an adsorbent. The kinetics of adsorption was studied and the influence on it of other parameters such as the concentration of the dye solution, the amount of the adsorbent, pH of the system was seen. The thermodynamic parameters such as change in free energy, entropy and enthaphy were caluculated using the above data. A probable model has been suggested.

Introduction

Textile dyes were found to be very toxic in nature. It is very harmful for living organisims if it is left as such in the flowing stream. Due to chemical as well as biological changes, there is a consumption of the dissolved oxygen which decreases the BOD and COD of water. It is therfore essential for the treatment of the industrial water before use.

Adsorption was found to be very important phenomenon for biological, industrial as well as environmental studies. Allen *et al.* (1989) have used simple peat treated under different conditions as an adsorbent for the removal of acidic as well as basic dyes. The other adsorbents as fly ash (Pandey *et al*. 1984), clay material, varieties of alumina (Ram *et al*. 1997) and silica (Khokhlova *et al*. 1990, Ram *et al*. 1993) have been used for the removal of dyes from various industries. Recently, the polymeric materials such as cellulose (Singla and Jain 2000) and poly aniline (Palit and Moulik, 2000) have been utilized for the adsorption of dyes and a moderate result was found. However very few studies have been carried out in the kinetics of adsorption. Therefore, the present study includes the kinetics of adsorption as various interval of time and rate was calculated using these data.

Experimental:

The nature of the adsorbent depends mainly on the chemical composition but the surface is equally responsible which affects adsorption because of the presence of the pores, edges, corners, cracks and pretreatment. Keeping these things in the mind, basic alumina was chosen as an adsorbent. Chromatographic grade basic alumina (active) supplied by Indian Drugs and Pharmaceutical Ltd. Hyderabad (India), sieved for the particles 100-140 mesh sized was washed with boiling distilled water, repeatedely till the complete removal of the impurities (if any), dried at 80-90^{0}C for at least 10 hrs. for complete dryness and finally used for the purpose. The dyes chosen for the study were basic brown and basic violet which are used in the textile industries. Due to unavoidable circumstances, the effluent was not collected from the industries however, similar solutions were prepared in the laboratory. The detalied procedure for the preparation of the solution is given below:

The above dyes were purified by dissolving in ethanolic solution and were-crystallized. Stock solutions (1.0×10^{-3}M) were prepared by dissolving weighed quantities of dyes in deionised water and kept them in the closed glass apparatus in a cool place. The experimental solutions were obtained by dilution as desired.

Kinetic Studies :

In the first series of experiments, the kinetics of adsorption was studied. For this purpose, 2.0g of basic alumina was kept in contact with a large volume of dye solution (300 ml basic brown, 200 ml basic violet) at a constant temperature in a thermostatic bath and at certain interval of time, a fix volume of the aliquote(3.0ml) was withdrawn for the measurement of the concentration by measuring the absorbance of the solution at a particular wave length. The amount adsorbed thus was calculated by the difference of the intial as well as the final concentration of the soultions. The expeiments were carried out at various parameters such as concentration of the dye solution, different amount of the adsorbent as well as pH of the system. The results are given in tables 1-3 and figs1 & 2.

Adsorption Isotherm :

In another series of experiments, a fixed quantity of the adsorbent was kept in different concentrations of the dye solution at a constant temperature till the complete saturation of adsorbate-adorbent system in a bath shaker. After that, the dye solution was withdrawn and the concentration of the soultion was measured as described above. For this purpose, 50 ml of dye solution (the concentration range of the basic brown 4.0-8.0x10^{-5}M; basic violet 1.0x10^{-5} to 4.0x 10^{-5} M) was kept with 0.25 g of basic alumina at 30^{0}C for 4 hours to maintain the equilibrium. The detalied procedure for the calculation is already described. The results are given in Table 4.

Results and Discussion :

Fig.1 indicates the plot of the variation of the dye uptake with time at different concentration of the dye solution. It shows that the adsorption becomes rapid intially and after that reaches towards equilibrium. Almost 80% of the dye solution is removed from the bulk in 20 minutes. This might be due to the orientation of dye molecules on the surface of the adsorbent. However on increasing the concentration of dye solution, an increase in adsorption was observed. Thus on increasing the concentration of basic brown 4 from 4.0-7.0x10^{-5}M, the amount of dye increase from 1.12x10^{-3} gg-1 at 30^{0}C. The other results are given in table 1.

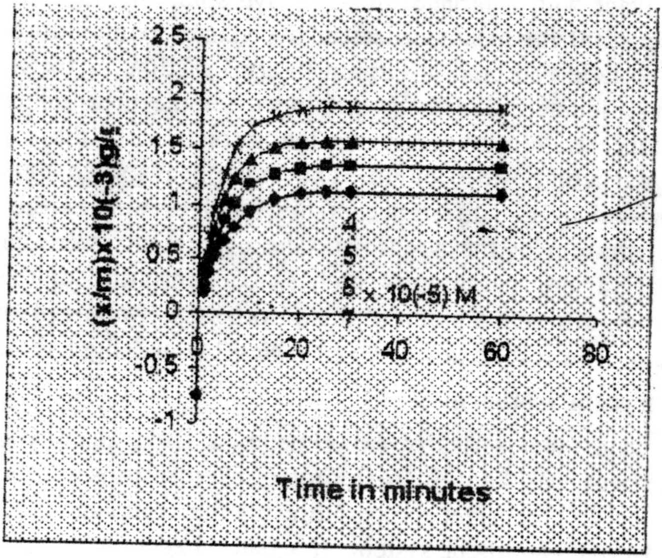

Fig. 1 : Time rate study of adsorption of basic brown 4 on basic alumina.

Table 1: Adsorption of basic brown 4 and basic violet on basic alumina at equilbirium, Temperature 30± 0.1°C

Conc. of basic *brown4* *(mole^{-1}) 10^5*	(x/m) 10^3 *g/g*	Conc. of *basic violet 2* *(mole^{-1}) 10^5*	(x/m) 10^4
4.0	1.12	0.80	1.43
5.0	1.35	1.00	1.76
6.0	1.59	1.20	2.06
7.0	1.89	1.40	2.35

On the other hand on increasing the amount of the adsorption was found to decrease. Thus a decrease in adsorption was found to be from 1.35 x 10^{-3} gg^{-1} to 0.85x10^{-3} gg^{-1} on increasing the amount of basic alumina from 2.0 to 4.0 g. keeping the conc. of basic brown 4 as 5.0x10^{-5} M at 30° C (Table-2)

Table 2: Effect of the amount of the adsorbent on the kinetics of adsorption, Temperature 30⁰C

System	*Amount of adsorbent(g)*	*$(x/m)x10^3$ g/g*
Basic alumina-	2.0	1.35
basic brown 4	2.5	1.21
Initial concentration	3.0	1.06
$5.0x10^{-5}$M	4.0	0.85
Basic alumina-	1.0	$274x10^{-4}$
Basic violet 2	1.5	2.18
Initial concentration	2.0	1.76
$1.0x10^{-5}$ M	2.5	1.54

This is indicative of the fact that adsorption depends on the active sites present on the adsorbent. Thus it can be concluded from the above results that the extent of dye removal from the solution depends on both the concentration of the adsorbate as well as the amount of the adsorbent. The straight line plot of -log (1-f) vs time (plots are not given) is indicative of the first order process, according to the equation

$$kt=-2.303 \log(1-f)$$

where f is the fraction of the dye adsorbed onto the surface at various interval of time, and k is the specific reaction rate. The values for the specific reaction rates are given in tables 1-2.

Effect of Temperature

Temperature is one of the most important factor, which determines the extent of adsorption of the given system. The experiments were carried out at various temperatures in the range 20-50⁰C for the above system. Since adsorption is an exothermic phenomenon, decrease in adsorption would be observed on increasing the temperature of the system. Thus the uptake was found to be decreased from 1.46×10^{-3} to 1.15×10^{-3} gg-1 in the case of basic alumnia-basic brown 4 system as temperature increases from 20-50°C (Table-3); the corresponding rates were found to increase from 0.184 to 0.227 min^{-1} respectively. The decrease in adsorption at higher temperature might be due to a tendency of the dye molecules to escape from the solid phase to the bulk phase with an increase in temperature of the system.

Table 3 : Specific reaction rate and energy of activation for dye adsorbent systems

System	*Temp. (°C)*	*(x/m) 10^3*	*Specific reaction rate (min^{-1})*	*Energy of activation (KJ $mole^{-1}$)*
Basic alumina-basic brown 4	20	1.46	0.184	
	30	1.35	0.196	5.64
	40	1.24	0.211	
	50	1.15	0.227	
Basic alumina-basic violet 2	20	0.199	0.089	
	30	0.176	0.098	6.37
	40	0.153	0.106	
	50	0.131	0.113	

The energy activation culculated from the Arrhenius plot i.e. log K vs 1/T (Fig 2) for both the cases were found to be 5.64 and 6.37 kj $mole^{-1}$ (Table-3) is indicative of the fact that adsorption is faster in case of basic alumina-basic brown 4 system than basic alumina basic violet 2 as observed experimentally.

Influence of pH:

The study was carried out by varying the pH of the solution from acidic medium to basic medium and the variation of adsorption with time was found to be same as described above. This shows that the adsorption follows first order with a monolayer formation on the surface. The amount adsorbed as well as the rate of the reaction calculated while applying the first order equation were found to increse with an increase in the pH of the system. The results are given for both system in table 4.

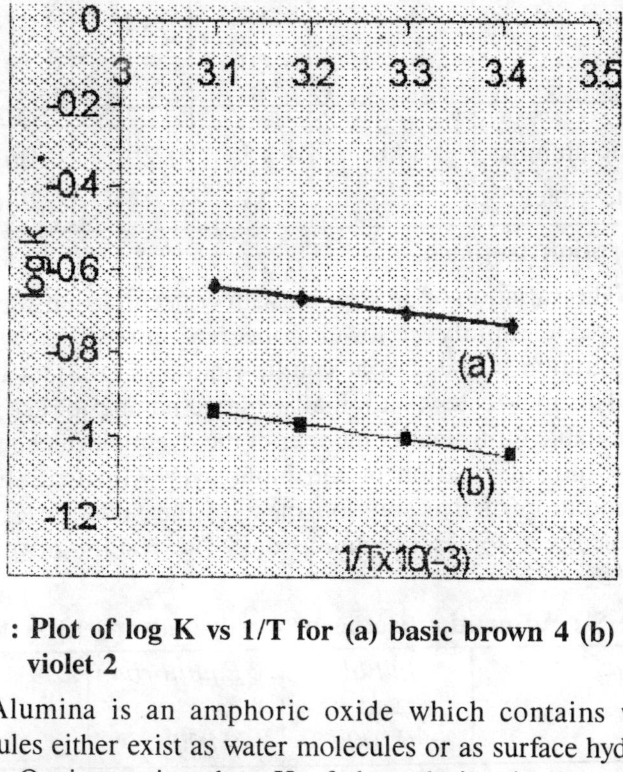

Fig. 2 : Plot of log K vs 1/T for (a) basic brown 4 (b) basic violet 2

Alumina is an amphoric oxide which contains water molecules either exist as water molecules or as surface hydroxyl group. On increasing the pH of the solution in the surface hydroxyl groups dissociated and a negatively charged surface is formed which is responsible for higher adsorption of cationic dyes.The scheme is shown below :

Surface-AlOH-------Surface-$AlO^- + H^+$

Dye + S-AlO→S-AlO^-[Dye^+]

In actual experiment, adsorption of cationic dyes by basic alumina is favoured at higher pH of the solution.

Table 4: Effect of pH on adsorption of dyes at 30°C

System	*Initial dye conc ($x10^5M$)*	*pH*	*$(x/m)10^3$*	*Specific reaction rate (min^{-1})*
Basic alumina basic brown 4	5.0	4.10	1.31	0.171
		5.15	1.42	0.186
		6.20	1.53	0.197
Basic alumina basic violet 2	1.0	4.15	0.202	0.061
		5.25	0.221	0.066

Adsorption Isotherm :

The variation of adsorption with concentrartion was found to increase rapidly at lower concentration while at higher concentration it reahches at equilibirium at a constant temperture. This indi- cates that initially a large number of active sites are available for a smaller number of the dye molecules resulting therby the information of the monolayer. On increasing the concentration of dye solution most of the sites are occupied and finally it comes to equilbirium. The results are given in Table 5.

Table 5 : Adsorption isotherm for dye-adsorbent system

System	*Initial conc. $(M)10^5$*	*Equilibrium conc. $(M)10^5$*	*X/m*
Basic alumina-basic brown 4	4.0	2.22	0.82x10-3
	4.5	2.46	0.94
	5.0	2.71	1.05
	5.5	2.98	1.16
	6.0	3.27	1.26
	7.0	3.88	1.44
	7.5	4.19	1.53
	8.0	4.52	1.161

System	*Initial conc. (M) 10^5*	*Equilibrium conc. (M) 10^5*	*X/m*
Basic alumina-	1.0	0.53	1.73x10-4
basic violet 2	1.5	0.65	3.10
	2.0	0.84	4.24
	2.5	1.06	5.28
	3.0	1.32	6.15
	3.5	1.64	6.80
	4.0	2.00	7.32

According to Freundlich adsorption Isotherm

$$x/m = KCe^{1/n}$$

Where x/m is quantity of dye adsorbed in gg-1 and K and nboth are constants dependent on the system. The value of n and K may be calculated from the slope and the intercept of log-log plot of x/m and Ce. The value of 1/n was found to be 0.355 indicating the formation of monolayer on the surface of solid.

The standard free energy was calculated using the following equation-

$$\Delta G = - RT \ln K$$

Where K is equilbrium constant between the concentration of dye present on the surface and the total concentration of dye used for the study. The change in enthalpy was determined from the slope of the linear plot of K vs1/T (plots are not given) and the change in entropy was calculated using

$$\Delta S^0 = (\Delta H^0 - \Delta G^0)/T$$

The results are given in Table-6.

Table 6 : Thermodynamics quantities calculated from adsorption isotherm

System	*Temp. (^0C)*	*Equilibrium Constant*	*Free Energy change -Δ G (KJmole^{-1})*	*Entropy Change -Δ S*	*Enthalpy Change -Δ H*
Basic	25	7.80	5.09	173.72	
alumina	30	5.00	4.05	174.29	
basic	35	3.45	3.17	174.43	56.86
brown4	40	2.53	2.42	173.92	
	45	2.06	1.91	172.80	
Basic	25	1.40	0.83	33.15	
alumina	30	1.31	0.68	33.10	
basic	35	1.22	0.51	33.11	10.71
Violet 2	40	1.14	0.34	33.13	
	45	1.07	0.18	33.11	

The negative values of ΔG^0 show that the process is spontaneous with a high affinity of dye with the surface of the adsorbent. A negative entropy change (ΔS^0) found in the present study is indicative of the decrease in randomness of the system. Similar results have been reported by Wright and Praft with adsorption of aromatic compounds onto oxide and carbon black.

Influence of electrolyte and surfactants on adsorption process:

Textile waste water usually contains sufficient amount of electrolytes both weak strong and surfactants as they have been used as carrier in the dyeing process. The aim of the present work is to find out appropriate methods and optimum conditions to remove dye from aqueous solutions. It is therfore planned to investigate the adsorption of dyes in the presence of electrolytes and the surfactants (Table-7) which is a favourable condition for the removal of dye from the solution.

Table 7: Effect of concentration of salt and surfactant on dye adsorbent system at 30°C

Conc. of basic brown 4 : 5.0×10^{-4}M

Conc. of basic violet 2 : 1.0×10^{-4}M

Conc. of KCl	*(x/m)x10^{-4} (g/g)*		*%of surfactant (CTAB)*	*(x/m)x 10^{4} (g/g)*
	Basic Violet 2	Basic brown 4		Basic Violet 2
0.0	1.73	1.05	0.00	1.73
0.01	0.34	0.96	0.01	1.37
0.02	0.06	0.90	0.02	1.18
0.04	0.00	0.82	0.04	0.88
0.08	0.00	0.71	0.06	0.78
			0.08	0.67

Conclusion:

On the basis of the above studies it could be concluded that a cheap material like alumina which is easily available can be used for the removal of the dyes from the industrial effluents within a short time. The thermodynamic parameters calculated from the above studies show the orientation of the molecules on the surface resulting thereby a larger interaction between the surface and the dye molecules.

REFERENCES

K.K. Panday, G.Prasad, V.N. Singh Natl. Acad. Sci. Letters (India) 6, 415, 1984.

R.N. Ram and B.B. Prasad, Indian J. Chem. 24A, 24, 1985.

S.J. Allen, G. Mckay K.Y.H. Khader, Environ, Pollution 56,39,1989.

T.D. Khokhloa, Yu.S. Nikitin, L.G. Garkavenko and A.L. Destistova, Khim Tekhnol. Vody. 12, 517, 1990.

M.N. Ahmed, Jacob Jhon and R.N. Ram J.Environ. Sci, Health 28, 1581, 1993.

M.Desai, A Dogra, S. Vora, P. Bahadur and R.N. Ram. Indian J. Chem. 36,938, 1997.

D.Palist and S.P. Manlik, Indian. J. Chem. 39, 611, 2000.

M.L. Singla and D.V.S. Jain, Indian. J. Chem. 39, 603, 2000.

22

Noise Pollution : Issues and Implications

Bindoo Bhatt, Divyang Trivedi, Jobi Charian and Pravez Vora

Progress in agriculture and industry is generally taken as indicators of development of any country. It has jeopardized the health of man itself. Noise has become a permanent part of our lives these days and is one of the most dangerous pollutant of mans environment.

Noise pollution is one of such problems need to be addressed. Noise pollution is unwanted sound "dumped" into the environment without regards to adverse effect it may have.

The present paper deals with noise pollution and its implications, a problems which have not addressed adequately. It also suggests the strategies of control.

1. Introduction

The persistent horning of a car stuck in a traffic jam. The blaring music playing at wedding in the nearly community hall. The loud speaker, music system and should emitting devices during festivals. The mind numbing splutter of gesets every time power breaks down, many many such examples. It gets to you make you want to plug your ears, mouth profanities, or helplessly scream in sheet exasperation. But that's about as far as most of us go. That it is irritating and anoying. It is noise pollution—the unwanted sound "dumped" into the environment without regard to the adverse effect is may have. Like several air and water pollutants noise has been accepted as pollutant under Environment Protection Act, 1986.

With rapid industrialization and urbanization , noise has become an increasingly trouble some community problem. Noise has become a permanent part of our lives these days because of development of machines, industry technology and is of the most dangerous pollutants of aman's environment. Again it may be pointed out that unlike other pollutants it is not an element, compound or a substance and thus it cannot accumulate and harm feature generations. There is no lag-time between its generation and its impact. It has instanteous effect.

The world noise is derived from the Latin word 'nausea' meaning a feeling of sickness at the stomach with an urge to comit. Noise has been considered as an unjustifable interference and imposition upon human comfort health and quality of life.

2 Mechanism

Sound is special kind of wave action usually transmitted by air in form of pressure waves and received by the hearing appartus present in the body of animals. Audible sound is one which air ears can perceive and a very wide range of frequency of sound wave is audible to human ears. The judgment of what sound quality and intesity is called noise is subjective. For example, a high intensity disco or pop music is very pleasent to those who are found and nuisance and unwanted sound to most people. In spite of subjectivities of noise some objective criteria for subjective human in speech damage to hearing, decrease in work perfomance, deficiency etc.

Sound starts a series of waves which moves by pressure generated at the time of sound production and carried through medium of propagation as distance increase. Thus high pressure sound can cause damage in number of ways on our hearing ability, brain and balaching mechanism. Beyond upper threshold level, the noise causes pain, damage to ear drum and oscillates and causes deafness. Noise and its impact on human dates back when 1964 Robert Alex Baron for the fist time pointed out that noise has damaging physiological and psychological effects.

1.3 CHARACTERISTIC OF SOUND

1. Sound intensity :

This is the amount of sound energy that flows through a unit area of the medium in unit time interval. It is measured in a scale called decible or dB scale. Starting form zero which is the finest sound of 115 dB. The loudest sound a person can stand without discomfort is about 80 dB. Beyond this it can be regarded as pollutant as it harms hearing system.

Who has fixed 45 dB as safe noise level as city. When noise level rise over 55 dB sound becomes unsound Mumabi, Delhi, Kolkata and Chennai usually register more than 90 dB.

2. Frequency

The rate of oscillations of sound measured in Hetz

Table 2.1 : Source of Noise with intensities

Source	*Intensity(db)*	*Sound level understood by common men*
Breathing	10	Very Quite
Soft Whisper	20-30	Very Quite
Library	30-35	Moderately loud
Normal Conversation	35-60	Moderately loud
Vaccum cleaner	70	Moderately loud
Telephone	60	Moderately loud
Food Blender	85	Very loud
Office noise	60-80	Moderately to Very loud
Traffic	50-90	Moderately to very loud

Motor cylcle	105	very loud
Jet fly	100-110	Undoubtly Loud
Train whistle	110	Undoubtly Loud
Drilling	110-120	Undoubtly Loud
Space & Rocket Launching	170-180	Painful

1.4 Sources of Noise

Noise may be broadly described as

1. **Transport noise** is includes road traffic, air jet noise, rail traffic nose etc. People living in cities are generally subjected to high level of transport/Vehicle which gradually deepens them
2. **Industrial noise :** Generally produced by industrial machines. Institure of Madras reported that hearing ability of one out of every 5 workers is damaged.
3. **Neighbour hood :** This includes variety sources causing disturbance and annoyance to the general public. Religious festival like Diwali-known as festival of light can now be identified as festival of sound "noise". This is true for any festival we celeberate. So sound so loud unbearable that it is important to understand its impacts like health hazards and defeating.

Intermittent and continues noises are quite annoying and causes fatigue.

1.5 Effect of noise Pollution

Noise can distrub sleep, rest, work and communication; it can damage hearing and evoke psychological, physiological and possibly pathological reactions (WHO).

Noise pollution or say exposure of human beings to noise leads causes a number of adverse effect ranging from mild annoyance, speech interference temporary or permanent noise included hearing loss (NIHL), mental fatigue, lack of concentration. Lower working efficiency, disturbed sleep (the effect of noise upon sleep varies greatly in young people 170 dB may wake them) but in older people 40 dB may distrub sleep Annoyance irritation, anxiety, strains stresses can change hormones content, produces body changes like increased rate of heat beats, dilation of eye pulps. Available evidence suggests that in animal it damages heart, brain, liver and produces emotional disturbance.

High frequency sound can affect the semi-circular canals of the internal ear cause nausea and dizziness.

Noise and Health :

Noise causes severe health hazards. Such effects may be physical or mental, which would have long term consequences on communication, working, efficency, personal comfort and can lead to industrial accidents. The physical health problems may be acute and chronic. The acute effects depends upon frequency 120-150 dB noise can cause permenent deafness. If a person is exposed to 90 dB noise for 40 hours week for say 30 years, he is bound to be deaf at the end of his career. A low level noise cause nausea, loss of physical control of hearing. The loss starts at a frequency of 400Hz, with more damage done by sudden impusive noises. The noise causes prolonged loss of sleep. The mental effect causes lack of concentration and mental disorientation. regarding communications, noise interferes communicability and causes proneness to commit error in judgement. The personal comfort no doubt gets affected, destroying peaceful life and enjoyment of leisure. it contracts blood vessel, thereby supplying less blood to heart and brain. it causes digestive disorder due to hyperacidity.

Behavioral Effects of Noise :

High levels of noise also gives rise to many adverse psychlogical effects. However even these are important in industrial situations, since they lead to lowered efficency, reduce output, increase absenteeism and higher rates of accidents and injuries. Excessive noise is known to produce behavioral disturbance such as annoyance, distraction, fatigue and speech interference. Low frequency noise at the lvels even as low as 50-60 dB can effect higher centers of the brain and can cause disturbance in the normal pattern and prevention of deep sleep. High level of noise make human beings more irritble and more susceptible to neurotic and irrational behaviour. This leads to higher rates of crime with the progress of urbanization.

Effect of Noise on Wildlife :

There is decline in migratory birds to a habitat if it becomes noisy. The Delhi Zoo Director has noted that animals, particularly the dears, lions and rhinos where affected from the traffic noise (1988). They become dull and inactive, and their health deteriorate. Similarly it has been reported that grixxly bears, musk-oxen and Kangaroo-rats fall victims to noise pollution in Maaysia.

1.6 The Status

In the industrially advanced countries of the world awareness about the problem of noise can traced a few decades back. They introduced both legislative and control measures. Motor vehicle Act 1939 and Industrial Act 1951 legislations Central Goverment under IPC noise pollution as a problem figure but all these legislations were vague to define specific standards and limits.

But it was only in 1986 through comprehensive Environmental Protection Act, 1986 in our country noise has become an offence. Fourteen year later in Feburary 2000 the union ministry of Environment and Forest (MoEf) formulated noise pollution (Regulation and Control) Rules.

Noise pollution is treated as part of air pollution and the CPCB is monitoring agency. With no documental proof noise levels exceeding prescribed limits it become difficult to nail culprits and the impact.

Table 2.2 : Prescribed Noise Limit

Area	*dB(A) Leg*	
	Day	*Night*
A - Residence Area	55	45
B - Commercial Area	65	55
C - Industial Area	75	70
D - Silent zone	50	40

Source : Noise pollution (Regulation and Control) Rules, Ministry of Environment

Note : dB (A) Leg-denots the time weighted average of the levels of sound in decibel on scale, which is related to human hearing

1.7 Conclusion

According to WHO report "of all essential problem noise is easiest to control" But the question of control uses only after awareness has been depending among the people that noise is a public nuisance and a danger to mental and physical health. Therefore control is necessary. People must therefore actually start making noise about noise pollution.

1.8 Suggestions :

1. Number of nosiy motor cars and other vehicles runing through residential area can be reduced by legislation.
2. Proper lubricants applied on wheels, machines. Silencing device in machines and vehicles could be made more effective.
3. Silent zone formation near hospitals and schools, educational institutes would be necessary.
4. Land use zoning for residential buildings should be constructed away from areas where outdoor noise land are high.
5. We must learn to celeberate festivals quietly without being sensitive about religion.
6. Suitable legislative measures should be taken to protect the public from noise pollution.
7. Controlling authorities need to monitor noise levels at regular interval and publish data.
8. Studies regarding impact of noise pollution should be conducted.
9. NGO's, students, organisation and responsible citizen should participate in creating awareness about noise pollution.

10. Educating the mass through news media, lectures and other programmes will go a long way creating a wareness among people of the need for control of noise pollution.

REFERENCE

1. Elson, Derek M. (1992) : Atmospheric Pollution: A Global Problem; Blackwell Publisher, Oxford, U.K.
2. http://www. 1hh.org/
3. http://www.dangerousdecibles.org/
4. Iqbal Muhammad (2001): *Environmental Hazards in Plant & People*; CBS Publishers, New Delhi.
5. Khokkar S.M. (2001): Envirfonment pollution Analysis; New Age Internationl (P) Ltd, New Delhi.
6. Roy Dilip (1998) : *Environment Management* with *Indian Experience*; A.P.H. Publishing Corporation, New Delhi.

Generic Index

✦✦✦

Subject Index

✦✦✦